People
Tools

People Tools

54 STRATEGIES

for Building Relationships, Creating Joy, and Embracing Prosperity

ALAN C. FOX

SelectBooks, Inc.
New York

People Tools™ is a trademark of People Tools 13 LLC.

This edition published by SelectBooks, Inc.
For information address SelectBooks, Inc., New York, New York.

First Edition

ISBN 978-1-59079-142-4

Library of Congress Cataloging-in-Publication Data
Fox, Alan C.
 People tools : 54 strategies for building relationships, creating joy, and embracing prosperity / Alan C. Fox. -- First edition.
      pages cm
 Summary: "Author presents strategies people can employ to build and strengthen the personal relationships he believes are the hallmarks of a successful career and enjoyable life"-- Provided by publisher.
 ISBN 978-1-59079-142-4 (pbk. : alk. paper)
1. Interpersonal relations. 2. Interpersonal communication. 3. Success. I. Title.
 HM1106.F69 2014
 302--dc23
                                        2013029442

Interior book design and production by Janice Benight

Manufactured in the United States of America
10 9 8 7 6 5 4 3 2

CONTENTS

This book is dedicated to Nancy Miller, who pushed me for twenty years to complete the manuscript, and to my wife, Daveen, who enjoyed the benefit, or burden, of my practicing People Tools on and with her for thirty-five years. Most important, *People Tools* is dedicated to you, the reader, with my hope and belief that it will add years of joy to your life.

FOREWORD

Craig R. Fox, PhD
Professor of Management and Psychology, UCLA

If you're still trying to decide whether or not to buy this book, don't waste your time on the foreword—skip ahead to the introduction. Or pick a chapter at random and dive in. Each entertaining segment delivers a nugget of deployable wisdom, mined from seventy-three years of a life well-lived and well-observed. But I warn you: find a comfortable chair, as the anecdotes will reel you in and you may have a hard time putting the book down.

My father is larger than life to many of his clients, colleagues, and friends, and I've often wondered where that magic comes from. No doubt some part of the Alan Fox mystique comes from his considerable business success, which enables him to live comfortably with occasional flourishes of extravagance and generosity. On top of that he somehow finds time to edit a poetry journal, oversee a charitable organization, remain connected with an impossibly expansive network of clients and friends, read voraciously, attend a surfeit of theater, music, and sporting events, and travel extensively. It seems like Alan Fox does more before breakfast than most of us dare dream up for our to-do lists.

But even were you to strip away all of the personal accomplishments and manic efficiency, I believe that my father would remain a powerful figure in the lives of those around him. Something about the way he comports himself and interacts with the people in his orbit seems to elevate them. A big part of his interpersonal success, I believe, comes from his skillful deployment of an ever-expanding array of "people tools."

I've certainly been on the receiving end of people tools myself. For instance, a couple of months after I began my first tenure-track job at Duke University at age twenty-eight, Hurricane Fran bore down on North Carolina where I had just purchased my first home. The storm ripped two dozen massive trees out of my acre of forest, badly damaged the roof, and shattered a multilevel deck. I was devastated and didn't know how to begin to clean up while I was beginning a challenging new job.

On hearing about the carnage my father cheerfully exclaimed, "This is wonderful news." I was stunned—it was as if he hadn't heard a word I had said. He continued: "Now you have an opportunity to learn all about working with insurance agents, architects, and contractors. Your lot will be more sunny and when you rebuild you can have exactly the kind of deck you want." My father's upbeat tone and forward-looking perspective caught me off guard. But I must confess that his response made me feel more than a little better, and it was the first truly constructive response I had received since the hurricane hit. And it was quintessential Alan Fox: optimistic, practical, wise.

My father's tool of moving on quickly from the past and treating each setback as an opportunity ("make lemonade") is a lesson that has stuck with me in the seventeen years since the hurricane. And his tool of embracing contagious optimism rather than wallowing with me in my misery ("smiley face") has since helped me to be more effective when supporting friends and acquaintances in pain.

Many years ago I served as an undergraduate research assistant for an eminent psychologist who would later win a Nobel Prize. One day I asked the great man how he came up with ideas for the many remarkable studies he had published over the years. Had he scanned the literature for gaps in evidence or opportunities to improve existing theories? "Not at all," he answered. "I view my job like that of a good novelist. I observe people—their patterns, their idiosyncrasies—and from that I form hypotheses that I test in my experiments. Only later do I return to the literature to see what has been done before."

I've sometimes joked that my father is a "pop" psychologist. The truth is that his fresh perspective as a non-psychologist with the instincts of a novelist have helped him to independently derive several important insights that have a good basis in behavioral science research. For instance, his observation that we can sometimes bring out behaviors in others that we expect ("self-fulfilling prophecies") has been confirmed in numerous experiments by social psychologists; the insight that prior actions are more predictive of future behaviors than are statements of intention ("belt buckle" and "patterns persist") also has a good basis in research; the notion that reward can be more effective than punishment ("catch them being good") and that we tend to overestimate how much others share our values and beliefs ("parallel paths") also have found support in scientific studies.

A few of my father's people tools are so keenly observant that they could inspire new research. For instance, in his chapter on "sunk costs" he observes that purchasing a ticket to an excursion should be viewed as buying an "option to go on the excursion" rather than buying the excursion itself. This subtle psychological distinction makes it easier to skip the excursion if one later finds a better use for the time—the rational course of action. In behavioral economics we call that a *framing effect*: people are more willing to walk away from an alternative when it is seen as a foregone gain than when it is seen as a loss. Thus, my father's idea to explicitly label sunk costs as "options" is an ingenious tool for self-management that, so far as I know, researchers have not yet formally investigated.

PEOPLE TOOLS ARE NOT ONLY useful for self-management. They can also be useful in managing others. A friend of mine who used to teach at Harvard Business School (HBS) tells me that the institution once surveyed its alumni and asked them what they learned at HBS that they found most useful in their lives beyond Harvard. Apparently the top answer they received from their alumni was "people skills." This accords with my own experience—I find that students typically enter business school hungry for quantitative tools of finance, accounting, and strategic analysis. Yet what often serves them best years later are the interpersonal skills they learn in a leadership or negotiation class that enable them to build better networks, lead others, and manage conflicts more effectively. Indeed, I often find myself sprinkling my father's people tools into my own lectures to appreciative MBA students and business executives.

The story is told of a new inmate's first night in prison. After lights out he hears the other prisoners shouting out numbers, each followed by maniacal laughter from the other inmates. The new convict asks his cellmate what is going on. "Oh, well, by now we've heard each other's jokes so many times we just call them out by number." Intrigued, the newbie shouts "Twelve!" but only hears silence. "Seven!" Only the sound of crickets chirping. "Five?" Nothing. Frustrated, the new inmate asks his cellmate why nobody is laughing. "The jokes are fine," responds the other prisoner, "but your delivery could use a little work."

Many of my father's people tools have been repeated so many times among his family and friends that we only need to refer to them using his shorthand labels. In the course of a conversation someone might observe that "patterns persist" as others nod knowingly. Or someone might say "watch his belt buckle" as others smile in agreement. To an outsider this may appear as inscrutable as the numbers shouted in the aforementioned prison appeared to the new inmate. But to those familiar with Alan Fox's people tools, his labels are a compact form of communicating and remembering useful behavioral insights. I'm pleased that my father is finally sharing his people tools with a wider circle of readers, and I look forward to the day when some of their labels enter more common parlance.

So what are you waiting for? Find that comfortable chair and dive in!

CRAIG R. FOX
June 2013

THE TOOLBOX: NAMING YOUR TOOLS

How forcible are right words!
—THE BIBLE
Job 6:25

Their villages were frequently [unnamed] ... if war took a man even a short distance from a nameless hamlet, the chances of his returning to it were slight; he could not identify it, and finding his way back alone was virtually impossible.
—WILLIAM MANCHESTER
A World Lit Only by Fire

When we experience joy in our lives, what else do we really need? This is the most important sentence in my book, and the reason I put it first. If you are like my mother you have already skipped to the last page to find out where we will end up. I will tell you now. The last sentence in my book is the same as the first.

While I was growing up my family always started dinner at 5:30 p.m. My father was a studio musician. He played the French horn for movies produced by Walt Disney, 20th Century Fox, and Paramount Studios, among others.

One evening he started our family dinner by making the following statement:

"Today I proved that my fellow musicians are unsociable. During one of our ten-minute breaks I stood against the wall with my arms crossed, and not one of them approached me to say 'hello.' Not one." There was a look of triumph in his eyes, possibly masking despair.

I was five years old then, and did not understand that if you stood against a wall, arms crossed in front of your chest and staring into space, that you were not proving your fellow musicians to be unsociable. You were proving that people leave you alone when you create a physical barrier and refuse to make eye contact.

As I said, at that time I did not understand this, so I spent the next twenty years of my life arms crossed, staring into space, proving over and over again that other people would not approach me. Dad, your system worked beautifully. It still does, whenever I want to be invisible.

By age thirty I was tired of solitary confinement, living in a prison of my own making. At the suggestion of a friend I enrolled in the Counselor Education program in the School of Education at the University of Southern California. I was determined to find the "get out of jail free" card for my soul.

I gradually released myself from self-imprisonment, but not in the way I expected. I realize now that I had intended to learn how to manipulate people better, present a more pleasing-to-others face, maybe uncross my arms and smile a bit. At the start of the Counselor Education program I had no idea that all I really had to do was to implement the simple strategy of being open and honest. A small change, but for me, nearly impossible. I was an attorney. Covert was my middle name. I was a CPA, much more comfortable with numbers than with numbers of people. I had started my own law firm and my own real estate business, and put a greater emotional investment into being "successful" than I did into being authentic. But, as a close friend asked me at the time, "Suppose they gave a life and nobody came?"

I realized I had to come out of my solitary self-confinement and make myself known. I began to learn, understand, and practice the keys to building fulfilling relationships. As a result I have enjoyed a successful life. Now I am sharing the vision and wisdom I have worked to accumulate throughout my life—those tools and techniques that I wish someone had shared with me when I was young.

During the past forty years my life has consistently improved in all areas. My business has prospered beyond what I could possibly have imagined; my capacity to deal effectively with a wide range of people has improved enormously. In short, I am enjoying all aspects of my life far more today than I ever have before.

So at age seventy-three here I am, grey hair and small pot belly, open and honest, and smiling most of the time. My wife, Daveen, is with me because I invented a People Tool just for her. Or should I say, just for me. To overcome her objection ("I don't date customers of my employer") I just blurted out my uncensored stream of conscious thoughts about why and how much I wanted to date her.

In fact, over more than thirty years I have used my education and extensive experience in psychology, accounting, and law to develop and practice a clear way of thinking, which I call "People Tools."

A "People Tool" is a behavioral technique you can use to change your outlook. Together they are like night vision binoculars peering into the darkness of your own motivations and actions, as well as the motivations and actions of others. The People Tool of Socrates will help you to know yourself better. The People Tool of Belt Buckle teaches you to look at actions rather than words to determine who you and others really are. The People Tool of Patterns Persist will enable you to predict with far greater accuracy how you or someone else is likely to behave in the future. After you read this book your life will change for the better. You will have a much greater understanding of yourself and everyone you come into contact with.

People Tools have been invaluable to me in building relationships, creating joy, and embracing prosperity in my life. I have accumulated quite a number of People Tools, and fifty-four of the best are in this book.

I hope that your life will be easier, and even more successful, than mine. So if your arms are crossed, relax. Put a smile on your face, open your heart, and let's get to know each other.

When I was twenty I thought about aiming to become a billionaire, at a time when there were only four in the world starting, as I recall, with J. Paul Getty. I figured out how much I could reasonably earn each year, what portion I could expect to save, and how many dollars I could accumulate from the investments which I intended to make. I watched carefully as my father invested in apartment buildings when I was a teenager, and calculated that if I devoted myself to money I could become a billionaire when I was sixty-seven years old.

But I questioned whether following this financial road map for almost fifty years of my life would be worth it. I wondered if the single-minded quest for money justified the sacrifice of family and fun.

I thought about the character projected by Jack Benny, a very funny man with a weekly radio show. For years Benny cultivated the comic image of being stingy.

The longest laugh in the history of radio came when Benny was approached by a robber, who stuck a gun in Benny's belly.

"Your money or your life," said the robber.

Silence.

"Your money or your life."

Silence.

Finally a third and insistent, "Your money or your life!"

Benny finally answered. "I'm thinking."

When I was twenty I thought about it, and decided that the money, even a billion dollars of it, was not worth my life.

At seventy-three I am pleased to report that I have accumulated more than enough wealth to satisfy almost anyone, and that I am not and do not intend to ever become a billionaire. I can provide education and medical care for my family, as well as unusual vacations to places like Antarctica and Easter Island. The bonus is that money buys time for me to enjoy my relationships.

One People Tool I use often is to Dangle a Carrot in front of myself for motivation. This entire book is a carrot to dangle in front of yourself. I hope you find it tasty and enjoy the crunch of discovery.

The story is told of a doctor, a priest, and an anarchist arguing about which profession came first.

"It must have been medicine," said the doctor. "How else could Cain and Abel have been born?"

"No, it was religion," said the priest. "It must have been God who brought order out of chaos."

"Aha!" said the anarchist. "And who created chaos?"

Chaos and uncertainty abound, and every day I use the People Tool of Sunk Cost to focus my life on the future rather than the past, to help me achieve the result I want—joy, a satisfying relationship, or wealth.

Although I could try using my hand to pound a two-penny nail into a block of Douglas fir, I would be considerably more successful, and my hand less bruised, if I used a tool, in this case a hammer.

When I wanted my wife, Daveen, to start a relationship with me I could have shown her my expensive house with a pool and view, trotted out written testimonials from my parents, or flashed my bankroll (held together by a large paper clip) in her face. I didn't think that would work with Daveen, and I wasn't trying to sell her my house, my parents, or my money. I was selling me—the real, scared, sensitive me.

I had asked her to lunch. As we sat down she said, "I can only think of two reasons why you've asked me to lunch. Either you want me to come to work for you, or you want to have a relationship. Which is it?"

Daveen always is direct. Thirty-five years ago I was often indirect, but in an act of divine inspiration I invented, on the spot, a People Tool to win her over. We now know it worked, and worked rather well.

You are already familiar with many People Tools and use them every day. The Sizzle and the Steak—you might already realize that in certain situations appearance is more important than substance. The 80% Solution—when is a person in your life "good enough"? No Before Yes—isn't it difficult to give an unqualified "Yes" unless you are confident you can, when necessary, say "No"?

With the various ideas introduced in this book, you can fill your mental toolbox with useful new tools and refresh those techniques that you already know, trust, and use. This is simple, but important and life-changing stuff. With the concept of People Tools you can employ your favorites in new and more effective ways.

A mother was teaching her young son how to cook a roast. "Before you put the roast in the oven you have to cut off each end."

"Why?"

The mother thought for a moment.

"Because that's what my mother taught me. Let's ask her."

The son telephoned his grandmother. "Granny, why do you cut off the ends of the roast before you put it in the oven?"

Grandma didn't hesitate. "Because that's what my mother taught me. You'd better ask her."

So mother and son drove to the rest home where Great-Grandma, eighty-nine years old, crocheted away her afternoons.

"Great-Granny," her great-grandson asked, "why do you cut off the ends of the roast before you put it in the oven?"

Great Grandma put down her yarn and smiled at his eager question. Then she whispered to her favorite great-grandson, "That's an easy one. When I began to cook many years ago the oven wasn't big enough to hold the whole roast. So I cut off each end."

Like her great-grandson, you might reappraise your old tools in light of new circumstances. At the appropriate time, you might consider listening instead of talking, or acting now instead of later (or later instead of now).

The People Tools described in this book provide a foundation on which you can build. The total potential supply of People Tools is virtually unlimited. And People Tools are free. You can easily invent your own personalized set of tools, selecting those which work best for you and eliminating those which are not helpful. You do not have to cut off the ends of the roast just because that is what you or your great-grandmother did in the past.

You might begin with the Tool of Imagination. Open your mind to the possibilities. You are unique. Your needs are different from mine. Your abilities are different. Your background and goals are your own.

Every possibility presented to you in this book can be expanded and improved upon, or you may wish to discard a tool that does not suit your personal taste or needs.

You are the world's foremost expert on yourself. After all, you're the only person who has lived with you for every moment from infancy through childhood and into the present. I invite you to blend your own knowledge and experience with the ideas which follow, and to discover, explore, and label many of the unnamed resources of your mind, as you fill your Toolbox with People Tools to build relationships, create joy, and embrace prosperity—in short, to build the life of your dreams.

RULES:
VISIBLE AND INVISIBLE

You never had time to learn. They threw you in and told you the rules and the first time they caught you off base they killed you.

—ERNEST HEMINGWAY
A Farewell to Arms

The exception proves the rule.

—PROVERB

I watched with interest when my daughter, Ingrid, then seven years old, followed the rules. When her first grade class was taught a song, she faithfully memorized each word. When the class was learning a new dance the teacher would say, "Watch Ingrid. Do what she does." Ingrid took her rule-following role very seriously.

When I was in first grade I had a more complex relationship with the rules. Because I was often punished for breaking them, I wanted to know what the rules were, not for the pleasure of following them or the personal satisfaction of doing a "good job." I simply wanted to know what the rules were to avoid being spanked by my dad, or sent to the principal's office by my teacher. Both of those events happened to me more times than I like to remember.

Not only was I often punished, but I was also often confused. I followed the rules but was punished anyway. As I grew older I gradually realized that society operates with two entirely separate sets of rules.

First there are the **visible** rules which are loudly proclaimed by parents, teachers, and religious leaders, and often enacted into law. (Parent: "Always tell the truth." Teacher: "Don't talk in class." Religion: "Thou shalt not kill." Law: "Writing a check for more money than is in your bank account is a crime, punishable by law.")

But there is also a second, parallel universe set of **invisible** rules, society's actual standards of conduct that even your mother will not divulge. All too often the **invisible** rule is the exact opposite of the **visible**. "In some circumstances lying can be helpful." Did your mother ever tell you that? Think of all the social situations where telling the truth would hurt someone's feelings and telling a white lie might be more appropriate.

And, of course, we often follow the **invisible** rules. Does everyone cross the street only at the crosswalk? Does everyone tell the truth all of the time?

The rules I have been talking about, both **visible** and **invisible**, are external. They are created and enforced by individuals and groups outside your own skin. But the full universe of rules is more complex and subtle than those that are external, whether visible or not. We are governed as well by internal rules, both **visible** and **invisible**. (**Visible:** "I want to lose weight." **Invisible:** "I have to eat as much as I can today, because there may not be enough food tomorrow." In this case I have a **visible** "want to lose weight," and an **invisible** "no I don't.")

The first People Tool on Rules is simply: Learn the Rules, both the **visible** and the **invisible**.

First you have to learn the external, **visible** rules. You probably already know many of them. These rules are taught in homes, schools, and places of worship everywhere. Many are posted on signs ("Stop" and "2 Hour Parking").

You have to study the motor vehicle code to pass the driver's license test, and also to learn why a highway patrol officer might pull you over. You might read religious texts to discover the visible moral standards of a certain group. You will ask a friend how early in the morning you can call to avoid upsetting him or her with an unintentional "wake up" call.

You also need to know the external rules that are **invisible**. These are more difficult to discover. They are not posted anywhere, but they are just as important as the visible rules.

For example, when I wanted to end a telephone conversation with my mother I used to say, "Talk to you soon." The invisible rule was that it was time for her to say good-bye. But my mother would always answer, "Oh, are you going to call me again?" She didn't know the invisible rule.

According to *The Wall Street Journal*, when Bank of America took over Security Pacific Bank there was "a clash of starkly different corporate cultures." Many Security Pacific employees were forced out. Kathleen Burke from Security Pacific was a notable exception.

"I sat down with a lot of Bank of America people . . . to get a sense of how the organization worked and what the unwritten rules were," she said. Ms. Burke became Bank of America's group executive vice president for corporate human resources, in part because she learned the invisible external rules of her new employer.

You must also know your internal rules. This task is complicated by the often enforced external rule which tells you, "Put the needs of others first." For example, if you have learned never to be selfish, you may have also learned to deny your own needs. Indeed, many of us carry this lesson to the extreme of not even letting ourselves know what we really want. After all, if you don't realize that you want to be alone for part of each day, how can you consciously miss your privacy? You may be plagued by a vague recurring feeling that "something is wrong," but unless you know your own internal rules you may never know what that "something" is.

You never have to defend to yourself your own internal rules. If you like onions with your sandwich, then you like onions with your sandwich. No justification is needed. None. You may choose not to enjoy onions with your sandwich to avoid the risk of offending someone else with your breath, but you do not have to justify your preference to yourself.

As you learn the rules, the second People Tool on Rules is: Make the Rules Visible.

While I was out of the office last week Melissa, my assistant, attempted to deposit a large check into my bank account. The teller said that the bank required my personal endorsement.

"But he's out of town," she said.

"Then just go over to one of those desks and forge his signature," the teller suggested.

Melissa did. The bank accepted the check for deposit.

This is an unusual example of an external invisible rule becoming visible. The visible rule is that if you sign someone else's name you are a forger and when caught you will go to jail. The invisible rule is that it is a perfectly acceptable business practice to sign someone else's name to a document if they would want you to and if no harm is done. You might find it difficult to believe this invisible rule because invisible rules are not advertised and they often are the opposite of the visible rules. We each must learn invisible rules from our own experience, which is often both confusing and painful.

You should practice making your internal rules visible. How much exercise do you prefer? I always tell a personal trainer that if I am pushed too far I will quit. And I will.

Some of your own internal rules may be visible (conscious) but many are not. You know that you love pizza because you eat it four times a week. That's visible. But when you are confused about what you want in life there are usually one or more internal invisible rules lurking. It is vital to make these ghost rules visible, to pour a coat of metaphorical paint over them, so that you can consciously choose either to follow or discard them. (See a related chapter entitled "The Belt Buckle.")

The third People Tool on Rules is: Follow the Rules, visible and invisible, external and internal.

Other people will act in predictable, helpful ways when you follow their rules. If you walk across the street in a marked crosswalk, automobile drivers should stop for you. Of course, there's another rule: look both ways. Remember the invisible rule that every driver may not follow the visible rule and stop for you. Recently, at a shopping center in Hawaii, I was almost run down by a driver who was backing up at a furious speed. My wife screamed at me to run. I did. I hadn't looked both ways. I wasn't expecting a car to back over me at thirty miles an hour.

The fourth and most important People Tool on Rules is: Break the Rules. To be followed the rule must be appropriate to the specific circumstance.

Sylvia, now a grandmother, tells the unhappy story of observing a rule that she now wishes she had broken.

When Sylvia's first child was born in the early 1940s, the best-selling childcare book of the day was written by Dr. Benjamin Spock. In his book Dr. Spock (no relation to Spock in Star Trek) recommended that parents feed their babies once every four hours, no more—ever. That was the external visible rule written in millions of books sold by an acknowledged expert.

"Often two or two and half hours after he nursed," Sylvia told me, "my baby would start to cry. He would cry and cry. He was hungry, but what could I do? Dr. Spock said to feed him every four hours. We tried everything, but sometimes my baby's cries were so loud that my husband and I left him alone in his crib and walked around the block to get away from his crying."

There were tears in Sylvia's eyes.

"I know better now. Even then I felt there was something wrong, that I should have fed my baby when he was hungry. But Dr. Spock was the expert."

Rules are a guide, not an absolute. Certainly there are penalties, real or imaginary, which may arise when you break a rule. But there are rewards as well. Those who threw tea into Boston Harbor flouted the laws of the British Parliament. Eventually they gained a new and separate nation. Teenagers routinely flout the visible rules and gain individuality and a degree of autonomy.

Often the rules conflict, as they did for Sylvia. When two rules collide, as they often will, you may have to follow one and break the other. It may be easier to obey the external, visible rule ("Feed your baby every four hours"). It may be more productive to follow the external invisible rule and sign someone else's signature.

If you fail to honor your own internal rules ("I should have fed my baby when he was hungry"), you may eventually conclude, as did Sinclair Lewis's *Babbit*, "I've never done a single thing I've wanted to in my whole life! I don't know's I've accomplished anything except just get along."

To summarize, the four People Tools on Rules are:

1. Learn the Rules, both the visible and the invisible
2. Make the Rules Visible
3. Follow the Rules, visible and invisible, external and internal.
4. Break the Rules, on an informed basis

The framework of your ideal life rests upon a structure of rules. The sooner and better you learn those rules, which to follow and when to follow them, the more likely you are to live the life of your dreams.

THE WASTEBASKET: DISCARDING STEREOTYPES

In the great blooming, buzzing confusion of the outer world we pick out what our culture has already defined for us, and we tend to perceive that which we have picked out in the form stereotyped for us by our culture.

—WALTER LIPMANN
Public Opinions

Helmer: First and foremost, you are a wife and mother.

Nora: That I don't believe any more. I believe that first and foremost I am an individual, just as much as you are.

—HENRIK IBSEN
A Doll's House

As a child, I adopted many chiseled-in-granite ideas about how an adult should live. A tablet of that wisdom included the following:

1. A couple should marry in their early twenties and spend every night together for the rest of their lives.

2. A good father plays baseball with his sons and takes his children to picnics in the park.

3. A woman stays home and cooks. A man handles the money.

4. If you're going to college, you have to start immediately after high school and continue your education without interruption until you finish.

5. If you ever accumulate a large amount of money it will eventually disappear.

6. When you praise people they lose all incentive to perform well.

7. Other people are out to get you.

8. Length of life is more important than quality of life.

9. Work is icky and should be avoided as much as possible.

10. If you are too smart, other people will dislike you.

Where did I learn these rules? From my family ("What's a mother for?"), as well as schools, teachers, and other children. In short, from the cultural stereotypes of my childhood.

My early beliefs were not entirely wrong. Quite the contrary. Many fathers play baseball with their sons and enjoy taking their children to the park for a picnic. Many women cook, and many men handle money. Some couples marry in their early twenties and live reasonably happily together ever after. But living by stereotype is treacherous because it often masks your own personal needs. One size does not fit all.

These ten particular rules don't work for me as an adult and, like Ibsen's Nora, I don't believe them anymore. Specifically:

1. I first married when I was twenty-one. Now, for more than thirty years, I have found joy in my third marriage, and admit that I enjoy an occasional overnight business trip alone when I can watch television as late as I want to.

2. I have two adult sons who are doing well in the world but I don't recall playing baseball with them. I do remember one or two picnics in the park.

3. My wife seldom cooks. We each handle money well.

4. Many years after completing my basic education I returned to earn a master's degree in education, and ten years later I earned a master's degree in professional writing. My wife started college when she was twenty-four and graduated when she was twenty-nine.

5. As a lawyer I discovered that many people die leaving a large estate. For them, their money vanished exactly when they did, but not one second before.

6. Praise motivates, criticism discourages.

7. Most people, including teachers, doctors, and friends, are actually out to do me good.

8. While the length of life is more easily measured, the quality of life is more important.

9. Work can be fun and fulfilling.

10. People used to dislike me not because I was smart but because I was obnoxious and sarcastic.

Gradually, over the years, I have discarded many of those "truths" I grew up with. I put them in my mental and emotional wastebasket, because they don't work for me anymore.

Yesterday I enjoyed lunch with a new friend, Hazel. She is thirty-seven years old, divorced, and described her relationship with a current male friend as "ideal."

"What makes it 'ideal'?" I asked.

"Because we only see each other once every few weeks. I'm extremely wrapped up in my business and don't have time to see someone every day. Or even every week. I know my parents view me as some sort of alien, but I like living by myself. I'm just not the marrying type."

Many stereotypes of "how to be" exist largely in our own heads. Today we "know" that smoking is bad for our health and that we should eat only enough to satisfy our appetites. Not too many years ago, however, we "knew" that smoking meant being grown up, and that we should finish every bit of food on our plate in order to somehow feed the starving children in China.

Some beliefs work for us. Some do not. Some we outgrow. I change. You change. The world changes. What satisfies me may not satisfy you and vice versa. Hazel likes to live by herself. I prefer to live with my family.

This is why we have the Tool of the Wastebasket—to throw out those ideas or values that do not work for us today (the only day we have).

For example, do you hoard money, or have you always spent every cent? Why? Because that's what you learned from your mother, or your father, or a peer? Hoarding money might be appropriate. Spending money might be even more appropriate. The question is, which of these tools will work better for you today?

Whatever your beliefs, act on what your judgment tells you is appropriate right now. Discard those "truths" that may have been helpful yesterday or those that might serve you well tomorrow. You can always change your mind.

A friend of mine, John, has suggested an enlightening exercise. Carry with you a small notebook and pen or pencil for one week. Identify as many erroneous "beliefs" as you can during that week. Write each on a separate sheet. At the end of the week you can read out loud, tear up, and throw into a wastebasket each "belief" that is inhibiting, false, or useless. You might want to do this with a friend and compare notes. You will probably laugh at his or her foolishness, and he or she at yours.

Build new, more useful beliefs. Throw your obsolete, rusty tools right into the Wastebasket. That's what it's for.

WALLS AND DOORS:
NO BEFORE YES

My unhappiness was the unhappiness
of a person who could not say no.

—DAZAI OSAMU
No Longer Human

"Yes," I answered you last night;
"No," this morning, sir, I say;
Colors seen by candlelight
Will not look the same by day.

—ELIZABETH BARRETT BROWNING
"The Lady's 'Yes'"

"**N**o" is a verbal wall. It separates you from other people. At times this wall is not merely a convenience but a necessity.

"Will you help me move next Saturday?"

"No."

"Would you let me get ahead of you in line? I'm in a hurry."

"No."

"Will you loan me five dollars?"

"No."

There are days when you may enjoy being a party animal. But on other days you may feel like Greta Garbo and "vant to be alone." You have that right. In fact, you have many rights.

11

You have the right to control the use of your belongings. You have the right to keep your possessions to yourself. You have the right to spend your money any way you want to.

Years ago I was at an NBA basketball game sitting in a cheap aisle seat. I was watching the players through my binoculars when a stranger approached me.

"Can I borrow your binoculars?"

She almost grabbed them out of my hands.

"I have friends across the way, and I want to find them."

Normally, I would have said "yes" and loaned the woman my binoculars. My mother taught me to always be polite. But a voice inside me said, "I don't want to do this."

"No," I heard myself answer.

"No?" She was obviously surprised. So was I.

"No." I was polite but firm. It was fun. And a little scary.

The stranger backed up three steps. Then she wandered down the aisle to ask someone else. I had erected a "no" wall.

I was pleased, but I was also uncomfortable because I had disappointed someone who might dislike me or disappoint me in return. I knew my anxiety was irrational, but an ancient ghost still whispered its out-of-date "wisdom" into my ear.

Yet I had the best of all possible reasons to say "no." I didn't want to. When you don't want to, a quiet, firm "no" should be enough. Your wall needs only to withstand a rain squall, not a hurricane. You do not need to shout, you do not need to convince, you do not need to justify a "no." You just have to say it.

My father didn't like to say "no." That's why his "no" was extremely loud and scary.

"I've washed the dishes. Can I ride my bicycle now?"

"Have you finished your homework?"

"Not all of it."

"NO!" he would thunder.

This is why my brother and I hesitated to ask Dad for anything. Each "no" was a cement wall twelve feet thick. Our distance was great.

In addition to the "no" that is too loud, but really does mean no, there is the "no" that means "maybe," and even the "no" that means "yes."

"Sally, I just got two tickets to the concert tonight. Would you like to go?"

"Gee, I don't think so. It's awfully short notice."

"But one of your favorite groups is performing."

"I know." She sighs.

"Do you have something else to do?"

"Not really. There is some reading I have to do for a class . . ."

Sally likes to be persuaded. She will seldom say "yes" easily. Maybe she's afraid to commit because she fears that she might make a mistake. This is why she usually erects a thin wall at first, but often opens her door later. Sally's friends find this confusing. Is Sally's "no" a wall or a door? I almost always choose to believe another person's literal words, so "no" means no and I don't go any further. Miscommunication leads to confusion. Confusion, in turn, ends in misunderstanding and mistrust. In this case even Sally's closest friends can never completely trust her words. They often give up when she wants them to persevere, or they persevere when she is really not interested. Does this remind you of anyone you know?

Most confusing is the word "no" that means "yes," an open door skillfully camouflaged as a wall.

"I'd like to throw a party for you on your fiftieth birthday."

"Oh, no. That would be too much trouble." (This is the "are you sure" variant of the "no" that means "yes," or the "show me how much I mean to you.")

"I'd really like to do it, after everything you've done for me."

"Well, are you sure it's not too much trouble?" (In other words, "Reassure me again," or "What will I owe you?")

"Not at all. I'll serve leftovers." ("You won't owe me much.")

"All right. But keep it intimate." ("I don't want to feel obligated to reciprocate beyond my own level of comfort.")

Even though many people engage in this type of indirect verbal sparring and label it "considerate," I respectfully disagree. If you want to say "no," say "no." Make it clear, concise, and consistent. You only need a modest barrier. Seldom, if ever, will your "no" require the Great Wall of China.

And if you want to say "yes," say "yes." Do not bewilder your friends by the "no" that really means "yes." ("Methinks the lady doth protest too much.")

And if you aren't sure, a simple "I don't know" is absolutely appropriate.

What about that Elizabeth Barrett Browning verse which introduces this chapter?

First, I suspect that her "yes" of last night flowed freely from her heart and permeated her being. As Lynn, a therapist I know, says, "This is the kind of yes to die for." Each of us knows when "yes" is true and complete. For example, you might read out loud to yourself the "YES" as proclaimed by James Joyce's Molly Bloom in *Ulysses*. (You will find that at the beginning of the next chapter.)

But what makes a full and complete "YES" like Browning's available? Nothing more or less than the possibility of this morning's "no."

To feel close, to fully give to or receive from another, you must retain the option to be separate, or even to change your mind. This is why I can truly open the door with "yes" only when I know I can later move behind the wall of "no" if I need to.

Saying an appropriate "no" can make you happy—very happy. Whether you are two years old or fifty, in using the word "no" you can take charge of your life. You will avoid people or parties that bore you. You will only give or lend money when you can do it gladly. You will not help a friend move if you fear you might end up in the hospital with a herniated disc in your back.

Of course, "yes" can make you happy too, especially when it is a full-hearted "yes," supported by your ability to say "no."

THE OPEN DOOR: YES

Whenever I find a human activity which works in practice, I immediately rush to my computer to figure out if it will work in theory.

—A Proverbial Economist

I thought well as well him as another and then I asked him with my eyes to ask again yes and then he asked me would I yes to say yes my mountain flower and first I put my arms around him yes and drew him down to me so he could feel my breasts all perfume yes and his heart was going like mad and yes I said yes I will Yes.

—James Joyce
Ulysses

"Yes" is the most powerful word in the English language.

"Do you love me?"

"Yes."

"Will you join me?"

"Yes."

"Can you help me?"

"Yes."

"Yes" is more than a word. "Yes" is a touch, a smile, a way of life. "Yes" bridges the abyss, responds to yearning, and makes everything possible.

"Yes" invites me to be close to you. It removes walls and allows the full flow of joy from my heart. "Yes" makes the whole greater than the sum of its parts.

"Yes" says we agree, you are enthusiastic, you and I will face the future together, aligned within an indifferent universe.

"Yes" invites a child into a world of sponsorship and safety. "Yes" admits an adult into a network of solace and support. "Yes" releases the unlimited possibilities of your soul.

I asked my brother, "Would you do me a favor?"

"I'd be happy to," he said.

"Wait a minute," I said. "How do you know you'd be happy to? I haven't even told you what I want."

"Alan," he said, "you are my brother. You've never been unreasonable in the past. I want to help you in any way I can, and don't want to limit my enthusiasm with a cautious, 'I don't know. Tell me what you want first.' I want to give you a loud, clear 'Yes.'"

My brother's "yes" was one of the best I have ever received. It felt great. I loved my brother.

"Yes" certainly works in theory. Does it work in practice?

Yes.

QUESTION MARK

*Ask, and it shall be given you; seek and ye shall find;
knock and it shall be opened unto you.*

—THE BIBLE
Matthew 7:7

Knowledge is power.

—FRANCIS BACON
Meditationes Sacrae

My friend Albert and his wife Alexis traveled to Milan, Italy, a city neither had visited before. Albert drove the rental car which they had picked up at the airport but he forgot to ask for a map and there was no GPS in the car. After half an hour Alexis suggested that they stop and ask for directions to their hotel. Albert refused and drove around, lost, for the next two hours. Alexis's mood swung between fury and resignation. Finally Albert had a brilliant idea. He hired a taxi to guide them to their hotel. He never did actually ask for directions.

This story is a cliché—men don't ask for directions. I'm a man, and I never used to ask for directions. Absolutely never. Maybe it had something to do with virility and I thought the hair on my chest would disappear if I asked. Maybe I didn't want to appear indecisive. What was my underlying motivation? Thanks for asking, but I really don't know.

In one of my favorite plays, *The Rainmaker*, the deputy sheriff is divorced and lonely. When he talks about his wife who left him he realizes that she would have stayed if he had simply asked her to.

What is missing from each of these scenes? The People Tool of Question Mark.

Question Mark means—if you don't know, ask. If you're not sure whether you know or not—ask. What you don't know may very well hurt you.

A couple had been living together for three months. Early one morning they woke up in a romantic bedroom on the beach at Malibu. She turned to him and said, "I'm sure glad I can't get pregnant by you."

"So am I. Uh, why can't you?"

"Because you've had a vasectomy."

"Did I tell you that?"

"Well, no, Sue in your office said you had one."

"You might have asked me." They each turned different shades of green and she was, in fact, pregnant.

Or the doctor says, "The result of the biopsy on your lump was positive. I recommend an immediate total mastectomy." This is the time for Question Mark. You should have many questions, including seeking a second opinion which I suggested to my mother when she faced this situation.

When is it appropriate to use Question Mark? Whenever you think that more information might be useful. Asking a question does not mean that you are dumb or lack education. It only means that you want more information. I will only be treated by a doctor who will fully answer each of my questions. My body and health are too important to leave to unquestioned chance.

I recently underwent surgery for a torn rotator cuff. Since I was told that my recovery for the first two or three weeks would be painful, I planned a visit to Egypt. I thought it would be better to suffer while traveling than while sitting at my desk. On the third day of a Nile River cruise another passenger approached me after dinner.

"I see you've had shoulder surgery," she said.

"Yes. The arm sling must have given me away."

"I've had three surgeries on my shoulders," she continued.

"Three? You only seem to have two shoulders."

"Three. My first surgery was performed by a local surgeon. It didn't work, and a year later I had to have a second surgery on the same shoulder. Later I had the same surgery on my other shoulder."

It turns out that she lived in a city not too far from me, and told me that her surgeon was Dr. Tibone.

"I hope he was your second surgeon, not your first," I said, "because Dr. Tibone was my surgeon."

Dr. Tibone was, happily, her second, successful surgeon, who later operated on her other shoulder. I guess she didn't ask enough questions of the first doctor, including how many shoulder surgeries he performed each year, and with what result. Instead of a second opinion, she ended up needing a second surgery.

Question Mark is extremely useful in getting to know someone. I always learn more when I listen than when I talk. A few of my favorite questions are:

"What is your heart's desire?"

"What are you most afraid of?"

"How do you know when someone loves you?"

"If you were to die tomorrow, would you have any regrets?"

When I was thirty-one and single I would always ask on a first date, "How do you get along with your dad?" (See Patterns Persist.)

I now use the tool of Question Mark often, and I have learned a lot. I must add, however, that there are ways in which asking a question is NOT an appropriate use of Question Mark.

Riddle: When is Question Mark not Question Mark? When it is a disguised accusation. For instance:

"Why haven't you fixed the toaster?"

"When are you going to get around to getting my shirts back from the cleaners?"

"Why have we run out of bananas? Again."

These are examples of how asking a question can be used to bully or intimidate, which I find to be self-indulgent and unproductive. I recommend instead the People Tool of Hold Me, which is to be kind.

There are other ways in which we ask questions that might not be an appropriate use of Question Mark. A few examples are:

"How much does your new job pay?" (Impolite, but I usually ask anyway.)

"Why do you like that dress?" (Could be interpreted as critical.)

Question Mark should be used to gather all the information you need before you make an important decision in your life, such as "Should I buy this house?" Use Question Mark liberally. There are no stupid questions. When my children were young and asked how to spell a word I always said, "I'm so glad you asked." Then I helped them to sound out the word.

"Why do you recommend a total mastectomy? Why can't we save something?" (Fear of questioning authority. As a result of a second opinion, my mother's mastectomy was modified.)

I suggest that whenever it is appropriate to ask a question you refuse to be fearful or intimidated. Don't drive around Milan for two hours before you find your hotel. There is a world of essential information out there, free for the asking, especially on the Internet. But you have to ask. Google or Bing will love you.

Be sure to use Question Mark if you want something. If you don't get what you want, ask again. And if you still come up empty, ask someone else.

Free yourself to use Question Mark, even if you're a man.

THE BELT BUCKLE

[The superior man] acts before he speaks, and afterwards speaks according to his actions.

—CONFUCIUS
The Confucian Analects

Words are wise men's counters, they do but reckon with them, but they are the money of fools.

—THOMAS HOBBES
Leviathan

"It's simple," the all-star defensive lineman explained. "The great ball carriers like Jim Brown or Gale Sayers fake with their eyes. They fake with their heads, fake with their shoulders, and some can even fake with their knees. But they can't fake with their belt buckle. Wherever that's going, that's where they're going. I just watch their belt buckle."

When I was young I asked many girls at my high school to go out with me. Since I was not every woman's dream date—all right, I was president of the chess club—my invitations were refused, often indirectly.

"Oh, I'm so sorry, but I'm busy next Friday night."

"How about Saturday night?"

"Let's see. No, I guess I'm busy then, too."

"A week from Saturday?"

"I really can't commit that far in advance."

I cringe now when I think of how many years it took me to realize that while her words were polite, each woman's belt buckle just wasn't going to head into my VW Bug.

Perhaps more subtle, but even more disappointing, was the Wednesday evening telephone call. "Hey, I'm really sorry but something's come up. I can't make it Saturday night."

It's human nature to avoid a situation you think might be unpleasant, especially, for me, direct confrontation. That's why words and actions often diverge.

I never knew whether a woman's Saturday night belt buckle was going to babysit, write a term paper, or park on Mulholland Drive with one of those darn football players, but after countless rejections I finally figured out that a whole lot of belt buckles would never sit next to me at the movies. I also figured out that they would probably be "polite" in rejecting me, at least to my face (or ear on the telephone).

With this realization I started down the path to understanding that words, including words of promise, are not the same as performance.

"The check is in the mail" is not the same as the check itself.

"I'll call you tomorrow" is not the same as calling tomorrow.

I'm sure that you have had similar experiences, and may have reached a similar conclusion. On a deeper level, which we may not even be consciously aware of, is the injury on both sides of the belt buckle. How many words can I slip out of by an opposite action before the sum of my small deceits takes its toll? How often can I dodge the truth of my intentions by saying to myself, "Oh, I didn't want to hurt her feelings," before I lose the connection with my own core? Before I become a living contradiction?

How many dashed expectations, raised by the promises of others, can I handle before I become cynical or withdrawn?

"A week from Saturday?"

"I really can't commit myself that far in advance."

And we each hang up the phone, and there's that crashing silence which everyone has experienced, filled with damage to us both because you have experienced your own crushing silence and your own words echo into it. Teenagers are so dramatic.

Why do we act this way? Why aren't we forthright, with our words and actions (our belt buckle) moving in sync?

It's clear to me that we avoid saying our own truths out loud because we fear rejection and we allow our own personal insecurities to overrule the silent truths that always live in our heart.

I want to rely on both your words and your actions, and I focus on your belt buckle because I want to be safe. I want to banish the unknown, and accurately predict my future with you.

About the rejected high school date . . . if both of us had been honest, who knows what rewards we might have realized? At the very least, had you rejected me gently, I might not have pursued you further and you wouldn't have needed to fear my repeated telephone calls. Openness and honesty may be too much to expect of a high school student, but, as teenagers, we do form habits which last a lifetime.

Of course, being truthful allows us to get closer to each other because we discover who each of us really is. Most people shine in that situation. Truth not only builds trust but also helps to heal past injuries.

Words not followed with the expected action can be hurtful. One such example involved my friend Susan. Her husband left a note on the kitchen table, which she found one evening when she arrived home from work. It said, "I haven't loved you for years, and I am out of here. Don't even look for me. Jeff."

Susan was devastated. She was unable to sleep that night. In the morning she telephoned her therapist, Dr. Offman.

"I am so sorry," he said after Susan explained her calamity. "If there is anything I can do to help, anything at all, I will."

"I need to see you today."

"Today? Oh. Today." Pause.

"As soon as you can. I'll come over right now."

The therapist was silent.

"Maybe lunch time?" Susan suggested.

Silence.

"How about this evening?"

More silence.

"I'm so sorry, Susan. No. Today I'm completely booked. Today is just not possible."

The therapist's words of promise were massacred by the reality of his rejection. Words are not the same as performance. Susan was deeply wounded, and told me that she will never forget that day, or that lesson. She immediately found another therapist—one who meant what she said.

My dad says that if you're willing to promise something you should be willing to write it down and sign your name to it.

I am grateful for my relationship with my father. Dad's belt buckle often rode in my VW Bug with me. In fact, he was there simply because I thought about him and felt his presence. Relationships are like that. They are always with you. Harmony of thought and action, repeated over the years, nurture strong relationships. We have the opportunity to know ourselves more and more as we make our way in this world, and injuries can heal if we are not reinjured by constant repetition of small or large deceits.

I sometimes wonder if, for a week, I should write down all of my promises. How high would that stack of stated intentions be, and how often would my actions match that stack? Consciously or not, we each wrestle with this problem. We can duck and weave, fake with our eyes, shoulders, even our knees as that opposing lineman looms over us, but the belt buckle always reveals the true story of who you and I are.

Thoughts are not the same as performance. How many evenings have I promised myself that I would write another chapter for this book, only to find my belt buckle plunked down in front of the TV set?

All of our thoughts, words, and promises may deceive us, but our actions are the true statement of our identity. We will always know who we are and what we want (or don't want) simply by observing what we do, rather than what we say.

I can be tricked by words, but I'm seldom fooled by actions. I think that's what Confucius and Hobbes are talking about.

Be careful, Jim Brown. I'm watching your belt buckle.

PATTERNS PERSIST

The more things change, the more they remain the same.
—ALPHONSE KARR
Les Guépes

Nothing is stronger than habit.
—OVID
Ars Amatoria

Whenever I visit a buffet restaurant I eat more than I had intended. This was true when I was twelve years old. It is true today, and I'm now seventy-three.

Patterns persist.

When I hired Michelle five years ago to be my assistant her references were outstanding. She was extremely personable at her interview and had earned a very high score on our thirty-question logic test. There was only one item on her resume which concerned me.

"Michelle, you've held a number of previous positions, but you have never stayed at any job for more than eighteen months. I like my assistant to be with me for at least four or five years. If I hire you, why should I believe that you will stay?"

I don't recall Michelle's answer but I did hire her, ignoring my own conviction that patterns persist. Did she stay with me for five years? Not exactly.

After five months Michelle's ideal job came along and she left. We remained in contact, and Michelle helped me with a few projects. On her new job she met and married her husband, but after about eighteen months (surprise!) she told me she was planning to leave that job. I immediately made her an offer she didn't refuse, and two weeks later we were working together again. Five months after that Michelle said that she preferred to work with another company. Again, it was "adios" for Michelle. Again, we have stayed in touch.

Patterns Persist. Persistent patterns persist persistently.

In 1991 my wife and I traveled to Hawaii to see a total eclipse of the sun. We stayed for a week at what was then the Hyatt hotel on the Kona coast. We found that the entire staff, from reception desk to bus boy, was extremely friendly and helpful. That same pattern has persisted in every Hyatt hotel we have stayed at since. Yes, patterns persist for organizations as well as individuals. A Big Mac tastes the same in San Diego or St. Louis.

When you try a restaurant for the first time and are met with poor service and mediocre food, do you go back? I don't. I assume that the pattern will persist, and I'm almost always right in this assumption.

Why, then, would you marry someone who is always late, expecting him or her to be on time for your wedding?

A friend of mine, Ed, badgered me for years to invest money with him to speculate in Treasury bill futures. He was convinced he could triple the investment, but needed my stake because he had previously lost all of his own money doing exactly the same thing. I agreed to open an account for $30,000 and split the profit or loss with Ed. It was an exciting ride, but in less than three months he lost half of my original capital. I grabbed back the $15,000 that was left, and haven't gone near the commodities market since.

Why would you entrust your life savings to the care of a forty-year-old stockbroker who isn't rich? Will he manage your money more profitably than he has handled his own?

Bernard Baruch was an extremely successful investor in the stock market. When he died in 1965 he was in his mid-nineties. Toward the end of his life he was often asked, "What will the stock market do?"

Baruch's answer was brief, accurate, and always the same. "It will fluctuate."

What are the lessons here?

1. Recognize your own patterns (Belt Buckle may be helpful) and expect them to persist. If you like the pattern, embrace it. If you dislike the consequences of the pattern either avoid the area entirely (I will never speculate in the commodities market again), work around it (eat in a restaurant which has no buffet), or intentionally try to change it (use a different People Tool than you have in the past).

2. Recognize the patterns of behavior in others. Expect those patterns to persist. At your twenty-fifth high school reunion you are likely to hear Sally's same annoying high school giggle, all the way across a crowded room.

3. Recognize the patterns of an institution or marketplace. Expect those patterns to persist. If you are interviewing for a job with a company which experiences high employee turnover, don't expect to be with them for very long.

Patterns Persist. Persistent patterns persist persistently.

SOCRATES—KNOW THYSELF

If there is anything that we wish to change in the child, we should first examine it and see whether it is not something that could better be changed in ourselves.
—CARL GUSTAV JUNG
The Integration of Personality

This sense of identity provides the ability to experience one's self as something that has continuity and sameness, and to act accordingly.
—ERIK HOMBURGER ERIKSON
Childhood and Society

If Socrates were an answer on *Jeopardy*, "know thyself" might be the question.

Actually that maxim, though used by Socrates, was already long established wisdom. In Egypt the ancient temple of Luxor bore the inscription "Man, know thyself" on the outer temple and "Man, know thyself . . . and thou shalt know the gods" on the inner temple. I trust words of wisdom which, for more than two thousand years, have survived war, famine, and literary critics.

In literature "know thyself" has been cited as an admonition to those whose boasts exceed what they are, and as a warning to pay no attention to the opinion of the multitude.

When I consider the large number of available People Tools, I wonder which are the most important. If you enjoy memorizing, then tackle the entire list. But in any specific situation how do you select an ideal tool or two?

To me, Socrates' "Know Thyself" tops the list. You have to know yourself—your likes, dislikes, abilities, disabilities, experiences, and goals—in order to select a tool, just as a carpenter has to know his project and his material in order to select the appropriate saw: jig saw, band saw, or hack saw. He or she would use different tools to produce a door than to construct a piano.

My mother visited museums in every city she traveled to, and there were many. My father preferred to sit in a motel room and watch TV. One day, approaching a city in Texas, my father asked my mother if she would like to visit the local museum with him. Startled by his sudden interest, she agreed. Together they spent several hours viewing the exhibits.

Later, in their motel room, my father said that he hoped she had enjoyed herself because he really didn't want to go but did it to please her. My mother said that she was tired, thought that he was interested in that specific museum, and actually endured the visit for him. Both my mother and father ended up at a museum which neither of them wanted to see.

My mother might simply have said, "I appreciate your interest, and normally would love to go with you. But I'm tired, and right now I'd rather collapse into a warm bed."

My father might have said, "I really want to please you by offering to go to the museum with you, but actually I'd rather watch TV."

When you know and express yourself accurately you will seldom suffer through activities which you don't like.

I don't like to attend weddings of people I hardly know. Daveen knows a lot of people. When we were married we agreed that she could attend weddings by herself, and that I would join her once every three years. By chance, at one of those weddings I met a man who worked in real estate, and we later joined forces in a real estate transaction from which I earned the largest profit of my career. Maybe I should attend more weddings with Daveen.

Each of us is unique. Your needs, life experience, and resources are different from mine, so we each start from a different place. It makes sense that often your choice of tools will be different from mine, which means that Socrates is the single tool which each of us needs to enable us to effectively rummage in our tool box. You have to know who you are, what you like, and what you dislike.

I used to believe that intelligence was a single global concept which could be reduced to a single number called "IQ." What could be simpler than the idea that a person who tests at 150 is "smarter" than a person who tests at 110? But I always wondered why people with a high IQ make so many dumb mistakes while those with a low IQ perform quite well in many situations. The explanation to this seeming inconsistency was published a number of years ago by the outstanding educator Howard Gardner, who, in his book *Frames of Mind*, concluded that there are seven distinct varieties of intelligence which he identified as:

1. Linguistic
2. Musical
3. Logical/mathematical
4. Spatial
5. Bodily/kinesthetic
6. Intrapersonal knowledge
7. Interpersonal relationships

"Aha," I thought as I read his chapters. I remembered Pam, an undergraduate at UCLA, who was a genius in social situations, even though her grades barely hovered above a "C." I have always been comfortable with numbers and in exploring my own internal process, but I blank out when I face a foreign language or, heaven forbid, when my car won't start.

Several years ago Daniel Goleman authored the book *Emotional Intelligence*, which makes a persuasive case for the proposition that there is a distinction between intellectual and emotional intelligence. Clearly, there are discrete domains of ability, and each of us is better in some than we are in others.

Regardless of your inherent ability, or lack of ability, in a given field, you can improve your performance in any one of them. I was a member of my high school chess club (which might say something about my social skills—I would have preferred to have had a girlfriend), even though I wasn't especially talented at playing chess. Over the years, however, I vastly improved my social skills. (Of course, I was starting from a pretty low base.)

How can you know yourself? Take a look at your belt buckle. What are your actions? My personal trainer works out with four or five clients a day, and in the evening visits the gym for his own workout. I would rather sit. I like to eat, often more than I need. My friend Jim has to think about when he last ate before he knows whether or not he wants to join me for lunch. I hate to offend people. The character Archie Bunker on the long-running TV show *All in the Family* didn't mind offending everyone.

I seldom enjoy shopping for clothing for myself. Once I was in a men's store with my mother and Daveen. After a little over an hour I said, "I can't do this anymore."

My mother said, as usual, "Just try on one more pair of pants."

Daveen said, "Mom, when Alan is finished, he's finished. He's going to leave now."

I know that when a voice inside my head says, "Stop," I have to stop. If I try on one more pair of pants I'll probably trip and fall, or rip the seams, or at best dislike the pants and reject them. I do not have to test myself any further on this. I know. Daveen knows. My mother . . . was my mother.

Next, think of previous experiences. What did you do? How did you decide? Did you like or dislike the result? Patterns Persist, but if your previous decision making is flawed in a given area you must be aware of that so you can change it. Have someone else make the decision. Whenever I come to National Boulevard in West Los

Angeles I always turn the wrong way. I'm very consistent about that. Now I ask my iPhone which way to turn.

Get help in discovering yourself. Ask friends how they really see you. Take a class, hire a therapist, read a self-help book. Oh, yes, you are.

Know thyself. Then believe what you know, and act on it in selecting your tool(s).

THE PICTURE:
FUNCTION OVER FORM

We do not seek for truth in the abstract ... Every man sees what he looks for, and hears what he listens for, and nothing else.

— GEORGE BERNARD SHAW
Letter to E. C. Chapman, 29 July 1891

It is the function of art to renew our perception. What we are familiar with we cease to see. The writer shakes up the familiar scene, and, as if by magic, we see a new meaning in it.

— ANAÏS NIN

In midlife my Uncle Morris changed careers. He stopped selling life insurance and began selling homes. I never knew him well, but one story about Morris is legendary in our family.

The first item on his real estate agenda was to personally visit every one of the 112 houses listed by his office. Wanting to save both his clients' time and his own, Morris interviewed each prospective home buyer at length, then took him and/or her to the two or three homes which best fit their stated needs. No daylong tours of a dozen houses for Morris and his buyers. This was an excellent example of using the tool of Efficiency, and I'm sure that Uncle Morris sold many more houses than the other salesmen in his office.

One morning Morris showed a prospective client his ideal home. The man loved the exterior, closely examined the kitchen and bathrooms, approved, then asked Morris, "Where's the basement?"

Uncle Morris pointed toward the ceiling. "Up there," he said.

"The basement is up there?"

"Sure. The basement in this house is right up those stairs. It's in the attic."

The prospect smiled. He wanted a room that could be used for storage and similar purposes, and realized an attic could work just as well as a basement.

Another sale for Uncle Morris, as soon as his prospect answered the question, "Why do I want a basement?"

This is a perfect example of the Picture. The Picture (function) is what you want. But if you focus only on the Frame (the packaging) you might miss the Picture.

I don't love salads. In the Phoenix airport last week at the perhaps aptly named Paradise Bakery, I ordered a walnut chicken salad sandwich on whole grain bread. As I was paying for my lunch I noticed that the menu included, under "Salads," the same walnut chicken salad. Aha! I was really buying a salad (the Picture) surrounded by two pieces of bread (the Frame). The prices were the same, so the two slices of bread were free. But essentially I was buying a salad.

The trap here is that we often fall in love with the form, the basement, and unlike Morris fail to realize that what we really are after is the function—a room for a particular use.

My brother always judged a woman by her appearance. Thin and young attracted him. For David, the Picture was the Frame. To him the form of a woman was her function. I find that personal characteristics, such as loyalty, intelligence, and liking me, are the Picture, and the body is only the form.

I'm not saying here that either David or I are right or wrong. What I am saying is that it is important for each of us to look a little more deeply than usual and decide for ourselves what is really the Picture, the function of what we seek, and not confuse the Picture with its Frame.

When you understand your underlying values and goals, you can find alternate ways to satisfy them, rather than being fixed on a particular solution. You can ask yourself, "Why do I want this?"

The world offers many Pictures. You have many choices.

PEOPLE
10
TOOL

THE POSITIVE
SELF-FULFILLING PROPHECY

The self-fulfilling prophecy is, in the beginning, a false *definition of the situation evoking a new behavior which makes the originally false conception come* true.
　　　　　—ROBERT KING MERTON
　　　　　"The Self-Fulfilling Prophecy"

My gran'ther's rule was safer 'n 'tis to crow:
"Don't never prophesy–onless ye know."
　　　　　—JAMES RUSSELL LOWELL
The Biglow Papers, Series II [1866] The Courtin', No. 2

Throughout my life I have made a number of prophecies or predictions about myself which have come true. Some are trivial ("I think I'll enjoy that movie"). Some are important ("I think I will like being married to that woman"). Perhaps my personal prophecies merely reflect my confidence ("I will succeed in . . .") or the lack of confidence ("I can't do this . . . "). Either way, they are often self-fulfilling.

If I attempted to walk along a long twelve-inch-wide wood plank I would have no problem. If that same wood plank was suspended between two twelve-story buildings I would be terrified and either refuse or, more than likely, fall. I am terrified of walking along the edges of cliffs or high buildings. Same activity (walking the plank), different prophecy, different result.

Tim, a close friend of mine, told me about one serious self-fulfilling prophecy from his first marriage. Tim had met his future wife, Marilyn, in high school when they were both sixteen years old. They dated, went steady, were engaged, and when they were both twenty-one they married. For the first seven years their marriage was excellent. Then, from Tim's perspective, their relationship deteriorated. After three years of on-and-off arguments—often the same one—Tim concluded one night that he wanted to let Marilyn know that he was at a point in their marriage that required a make or break conversation. He felt that he needed to get her attention, and chose his words carefully.

As Tim tells it, they were sitting in the front seat of their old Pontiac and he said to Marilyn, "I'm thinking of leaving you."

Tim did not say he was actually leaving because there was still an open question in his mind. He did want to let Marilyn know that their problems were continuing, and bothered him a lot.

Tim said he will always remember her immediate reply, which shocked him. "I've always expected this."

"I've always expected this"? After five years of almost exclusively dating each other, more than ten years of marriage, after three children, after thirteen years of mutual loyalty, "I've always expected this"?

Tim was stunned.

Later he realized that Marilyn had been living for many years with a scary self-fulfilling prophecy—that Tim would eventually leave her. Perhaps she felt inadequate in some way. She may have been filled with the memory of her father, who was unreliable. I never asked. But Marilyn's prophecy did come true. Tim told me that he wished her unconscious forecast had been that they would always be together because there might have been a happier result.

By comparison, I visited a psychic years ago. I was concerned about three important business deals.

The psychic told me that all three would fail. Please note that this was her prophecy, not mine. I responded to her prediction by deciding to be even more careful and to pay more attention to each transaction. My prophecy, which turned out to be self-fulfilling, was that all three would succeed, and they did.

I realize that few, if any, of us ever want to be wrong, and it is easier to fail than to succeed. So when you predict failure you might be right more often than when you predict success. In my mind, however, the real question is this: which prophecy will help you to succeed more often? That is the entire thrust of this book. That is the purpose of People Tools: to help you succeed more often. And I want to be right every single time just as much as you do. I know that when I predict failure or uncertainty for myself I am often accurate. But when I predict success, I am also often correct.

If prophecies tend to be self-fulfilling, I prefer to infuse them with optimism. I would rather succeed than correctly predict my failure.

BUY A TICKET

Early on Sunday morning Joseph ascended to the mountaintop.

"Oh, Lord," he prayed, "I have honored you all of my life and until now I have asked you for nothing in return. Please, Lord, let me win the lottery."

Joseph returned home and waited. The next Sunday morning he trudged up to the mountaintop again.

"Oh, Lord," he prayed, "I have honored you all of my life and until last Sunday I have asked you for nothing in return. I have lost my job and my children will soon starve. Please, Lord, let me win the lottery."

Joseph returned home and waited. The next Sunday morning, for the third time, he lumbered up the mountain.

"Oh, Lord," he prayed, "I have honored you all of my life and until two weeks ago I have asked you for nothing in return. I have lost my job and my children have had nothing to eat for three days. My wife is sick and needs medicine, which I can't afford. Please, Lord, just this one time, for my family—let me win the lottery."

Lightning crashed, hail pelted Joseph's head, and he was staggered to hear a thundering voice on high.

"Joseph—meet me halfway. Buy a ticket."

This morning I was retelling this story to my wife. She told me that Carol, a friend of hers, had been fasting for a week as part of a church group effort to help a member of the congregation, Paul, find a job. But Carol stopped fasting yesterday when she discovered that Paul was not even trying to find job interviews.

I used to wish that I could sit all day in my living room and two events would happen:

1. The postman would deliver money to me—lots of money.

2. The most attractive woman I could ever imagine would knock on my front door and tell me she wanted me.

I'm sure you're not surprised when I reveal that neither fantasy has happened yet. In fact, I've abandoned the idea that either one ever will.

After my mother died, my father's telephone rang constantly. Friends brought casseroles for dinner, offered their condolences, and invited him to visit. But one Monday morning three months later my own telephone rang. It was Dad.

"No one has called me for a week," he complained. "I guess I never realized it, but your mother always made our social arrangements. People really liked her."

Fortunately, Dad "bought a ticket." He began to initiate telephone contact with his friends. He located and attended duplicate bridge games, and he learned how to use the chat feature on the Internet. He has made many new friends and is dating several women. This is pretty good for a man who is a full generation older than I am.

If you really want to win the lottery, or attend a concert, Buy a Ticket.

PEOPLE 12 TOOL

TARGET PRACTICE

Climb high
Climb far
Your goal the sky
Your aim the star.

—INSCRIPTION ON HOPKINS MEMORIAL STEPS
Williams College, Williamstown, Massachusetts

I shot an arrow into the air,
It came to earth, I knew not where.

—HENRY WADSWORTH LONGFELLOW
"The Arrow and the Song"

When I visited my son Craig at Stanford University his friend Bertram lured me into a game of darts in the student lounge. Our target was the typical small dartboard. Although I won the first game, Bertram won the next two. In fact, after my initial "beginner's luck," many of my darts bounced helplessly off the wall.

Any goal in life is a target. I want the job. I want an invitation to the party. I want to win the game. Often when the goal is especially important the target seems to shrink to a tiny dot, much like the apple resting upon the head of his young son as William Tell was forced by the Austrian governor to prove his prowess with a bow and arrow.

You can either approach archery the hard way, like William Tell, or the easy way. The hard way is to practice, practice, practice,

47

taking greater and greater risks under more and more challenging conditions. Certainly practice and challenge are useful tools. But there is another type of Target Practice, which yields a bountiful harvest. Expand your target.

When I think about Target Practice I see my target becoming larger. Instead of using a minuscule bull's-eye I aim at a target as big as an IMAX screen. This kind of Target Practice produces even more bull's-eyes than Bertram made in winning our second two games of darts.

How can you expand your target? Simply make your goal more and more general.

When I met Jerry he was thirty-one, divorced, and desperately seeking to meet a twenty-five year old woman, fall in love, get married, and have three children—boy, girl, boy. The woman had to be at least five feet six inches tall, never married, and successful in her career but willing to give it up and stay home with their children.

Jerry was aiming at a rather small target. As months became years Jerry dated more than thirty different women. Most of them were tall, never married, and successful in their careers. None was willing to marry Jerry, have three children, and abandon her career to stay home with their as yet unborn family.

One day a very excited Jerry called me.

"I want you to meet Jan," he said. "Can you and Daveen have dinner with us Saturday night?"

I checked my calendar. "We'd love to."

As we were driving home after a lively evening, Daveen was surprised.

"I thought that Jerry only dated women who were five feet six inches or taller," she said. "Jan is shorter than I am. She couldn't have been more than five foot two."

"I think you're right."

"And there is no way in the world that woman is going to give up her $200,000 a year TV production job to stay home with babies."

"True. In fact she said that she wasn't sure she wanted more than one child, two at most," I added.

"What happened to Jerry's checklist?" she asked.

"I don't know. I'll ask him."

The next day I called Jerry.

"Daveen and I enjoyed our dinner with you and Jan."

"Yeah, isn't she terrific? I think we might get engaged."

"That's great, Jerry, but I thought you were looking for a taller woman who would stay home with your three unborn children . . ."

"That was two years ago," he said. "Time has worn me down, thank goodness."

"So you're willing to settle?"

"No way. I've just expanded my horizons."

"Jerry, you're going to have to explain that one to me."

"Sure. It's true that I used to be very particular about who I dated. I carried around in my head a catalogue of virtues, like a spec sheet for a new car, and if a woman didn't meet all the qualifications I wouldn't even ask for her phone number. But it didn't work."

"Not enough candidates?"

"No. I met a number of great women, but I began to realize that my requirements were too restrictive. I mean, five foot six, five foot ten, five foot two—what difference does it really make?"

"None to me, but you're in charge of your life."

"Exactly. I learned that what I really wanted was someone who is fun to be with, a good companion, and someone who adores me." (Aha! Function over form.)

"Jan certainly seemed to meet those requirements."

"You bet." I could feel Jerry's enthusiasm over the phone. "As I said, I just broadened my horizons."

Target Practice. Expand your target.

Instead of saying, "On my next birthday I'm going to fly to Las Vegas with Bill, Terrie, and Lisa, reserve a suite at the Mirage, and win $5,000 at blackjack," why not say, "On my next birthday I'm going to have a lot of fun"?

There is a saying, sometimes attributed to John Lennon: "Life is what happens to you while you're busy making other plans."

I was speaking the other day with Carol, a highly successful businesswoman who owns her own property management company.

"You know," she said, "I love what I do, but I never thought I'd spend my life in this profession. Do you know any five-year-old who says, 'When I grow up I'm going to be a property manager'?"

I don't. Nor do I know anyone who, forty years ago, thought they would be a computer programmer.

Each of us comes to earth—we know not where—so we might as well enjoy wherever it is we have landed. As Stephen Stills titled his hit song of 1970, "Love the One You're With."

Target Practice.

THE 80% SOLUTION

I can't get no satisfaction.

—MICK (MICHAEL PHILIP) JAGGER and KEITH RICHARDS
"Satisfaction"

I got the Weary Blues
And I can't be satisfied.

—LANGSTON HUGHES
"The Weary Blues"

Harvey and I have worked together on real estate for more than forty years. Several years after we met, another friend told me he knew a different real estate broker who was excellent, and asked if I would be interested in meeting him with an eye toward replacing Harvey.

I always aim to improve my business and my life, so I gave serious thought to that question. I mentally listed Harvey's strengths and weaknesses and I compared that list with my vision of perfection. Harvey's score was close to 87%. Not perfect (who is?) but quite high. After reflecting for a few days I called my friend and told him that I was very happy with Harvey and didn't care to meet a possible replacement.

The overriding thought which led to my conclusion was this: if a person meets 80% of my ideal, then I will stick with him or her and will not spend one second thinking about a replacement. A later refinement of that thought is that if their "score" is between 60% and

79%, I could be out looking. Below 60%—get him or her out of my life, the sooner the better.

I hope that the benefit of this approach is clear to you. After all, life is always a question of alternatives. Is your spouse perfect? Not if you've lived with him or her for more than a few days. The proper question isn't, "Is he or she perfect?" The useful question: "Is he or she good enough?" And if he or she is good enough, then magnify his or her positives and minimize their less important negatives. (Make Lemonade.)

I have a theory in that regard. Despite the fact that I grew up with the idea that my "one and only" was somewhere out there, and that my only task was to find her, I now believe that in this world there are at least ten thousand women with whom I could be perfectly happy. But I have no idea where Daveen falls on the list of potential great wives. Is she number one? Unlikely. Number ten thousand? Unlikely. She is almost certainly somewhere in between the top and the bottom. I will never know Daveen's exact ranking because it is impossible for me to meet, know, and compare each of those ten thousand possibilities. So I need to have a better method of deciding when I should stop looking for the perfect, and enthusiastically embrace the 80%.

The 80% Solution works. If your score is 80%, that is plenty good enough for me. (See also Shrink the Glass.) Granted, this method is entirely subjective, but what in your life isn't? Your 80% might not be my 80%, but it is your 80% and that is what is important to you. Maybe you are more picky than I am and will only settle for a (subjective) score of 90%. Good luck with that! Maybe you're more laid back than I am, and 70% is fine for you. No problem. Maybe you prefer a different score for different situations. Live it up, create a matrix. The important point is to pick a number, or numbers, and live with it, or them.

The 80% Solution can be applied to many parts of your life. Everything considered, does your job score 80% or more in your mind? If it's only 40%, what is preventing you from getting the heck out?

My cousin Laura called me last week. "I want a divorce," she said.
"Laura, you called me ten years ago and told me the same thing."
"I know. But this time I mean it."
"So leave him, Laura."
Pause. "But I like to interact with someone when I get home at night."

Maybe "someone to interact with" was worth 80% all by itself. More likely, Laura is using a different scoring system than I am, and will accept a pretty low score because she fears the unknown.

One final thought—how do you score yourself? Are you at or above 80% of your ideal for yourself? Think about it. You can't very well eliminate yourself from your life, so your task here is to bring your own score up to 80%. If you're not quite there yet, the easy way is to lower your expectations for yourself (Shrink the Glass). The other way is to improve yourself, and I'm confident you can get to 80% simply by using the tools in this book.

SHRINK THE GLASS

Life's but a walking shadow, a poor player
That struts and frets his hour upon the stage
And then is heard no more, it is a tale
Told by an idiot, full of sound and fury,
Signifying nothing.

—WILLIAM SHAKESPEARE
Macbeth V

Pessimism, when you get used to it,
is just as agreeable as optimism.

—ENOCH ARNOLD BENNETT
Things That Have Interested Me

They say an optimist sees the glass as half full, while the pessimist sees the same glass as half empty.

Recently I asked an engineer about this hypothetical glass. His answer? The glass is twice as big as it needs to be.

I'll go with the engineer, and shrink the glass so that it is, in fact, full. I don't have to be either a pessimist or an optimist. I just want to be happy.

Until he died a number of years ago, I always had mixed feelings when I attended a movie with my brother. I pay for admission to a movie in order to enjoy myself, and I usually succeed. I ask friends what they like, I read the reviews, and I select only movies that I think will at least keep me awake. (No horror films for me, unless they're *Silence of the Lambs*.) When a movie meets my 80% rule I walk out of the theater very happy. Between 60% and 79%, it's OK. Lower than 60%, I probably disappeared before it did.

David was different. Almost every time we exited the theater he would complain about some part of the movie.

"The music was intrusive." "Boy, the titles were awful." "Did you notice the lapse in continuity when . . ." These were a few of his extensive repertoire of negative comments.

When David watched a movie he wanted to prove that he was superior to the filmmaker. But David's disapproval diminished my enjoyment of the movie, and I suspect that his attitude reduced his own enjoyment as well.

If you are at an event, say the wedding of someone you hardly know, and aren't enjoying yourself very much, just Shrink the Glass. Reduce your expectations, focus on the flowers or whatever you do enjoy, squeeze out of your mind whatever you don't like so that your brain (the glass in this case) will be not only full, but full of whatever it is that you like. (I am writing this at a daylong continuing education seminar which is rather boring, but I feel that my glass is full because I'm working on a project—this book—which is important to me and fun to write.)

To me life is a succession of experiences. Our task is to make those experiences as pleasant for ourselves as we can. Those experiences are what they are. Our reaction to those experiences is subjective, and largely within our control. The water in your glass is fixed. The size of your glass is entirely up to you.

SUNK COST

Our joys as winged dreams do fly;
Why then should sorrow last?
Since grief but aggravates thy loss,
Grieve not for what is past.

—THOMAS PERCY from fragments of ancient ballads in Shakespeare
The Friar of Orders Gray

"I am the Ghost of Christmas Past."
"Long past?" inquired Scrooge . . .
"No. Your past."

—CHARLES DICKENS
A Christmas Carol

I was exposed to a number of valuable ideas in business school, many years ago. Some ideas made sense immediately. Some took a long time and much experience to sink in. One of those lessons, which certainly is correct but is not always emotionally easy to apply, is the "Sunk Cost Theory." It goes like this:

Yesterday you installed a new machine on your factory floor. It cost a million dollars. It will produce one hundred widgets an hour for one dollar each. Today a salesperson is trying to sell you yet another machine to replace the one that just started working for you today. The cost is another million dollars, but it will produce two hundred widgets an hour for a cost of twenty-five cents each. You can sell all of the widgets either machine can produce at a net price of two dollars per widget. You can run either machine twenty-four hours a day. Should you purchase the new machine?

Sunk Cost Theory says, "The cost of the old machine is entirely irrelevant. It's a sunk cost. The money is spent. It's gone. Forget it. The only relevant question today is, 'Can you earn a greater future profit from the machine you have, or from a new one.'" It makes no difference if your present machine was installed today or fifty years ago. You only have to consider the future.

I'll do the math. Working round the clock for 365 days a year the new machine will earn an annual net gross profit of $3,066,000. The old machine would earn an annual gross profit $876,000. That's an additional annual gross profit of more than $2,000,000. The new machine would pay back its entire cost in less than six months. My next question to the salesman would be, "How soon can the new machine be installed?"

If you don't believe and practice the Sunk Cost Theory you will limit, perhaps seriously, both your success in business and your success in life.

I won't talk any further about sunk cost in business. Although sunk cost does matter in business, it's even more important in your life. Suppose you've poured ten years of your life into a job in which you feel underpaid and underappreciated. You hate going to work. Is there another job you could find, another company you could work for, which would give you a greater emotional return on your time? (As Napoleon Bonaparte once said, "Go, sir, gallop, and don't forget that the world was made in six days. You can ask me for anything you like, except time.") Take a college course, go back to school, prepare for a new position. What are you waiting for? If your past investment isn't working for you, find a better alternative for the future. In business the salesperson may call on you. In your life you have to be the salesman for yourself. (Buy a Ticket.)

How about a relationship? My brother David pursued a woman, let's call her Sheila, for more than a year. He begged her to move into his house. He paid her $1,000 a month to work for him even though she did almost nothing. He helped her in every way possible because, I believe, he loved her. She did not respond romantically, and eventually found a job in another city and moved away. David continued to pursue her by long distance, entirely without success. His investment in a relationship with Sheila was enormous. His return on that investment, in terms of reciprocity, was zero. David didn't apply Sunk Cost.

My friend Bob has an even more serious case. He has pursued a woman, let's call her Ruth, for more than fifteen years. As far as I know they live separately but Bob pays all of her expenses—about $85,000 a year. A few years ago Bob confided in me, "I think she's playing me for a fool, but each time I'm about to give up she calls and invites me to dinner. She has a sixth sense about how to keep me hoping." ("Does the imagination dwell the most, upon a woman won or a woman lost?" William Butler Yeats.)

I might not go as far as Dante ("Abandon all hope, ye who enter here"), but goodness, Bob. You've spent more than a quarter of your life increasing a sunk cost. Move on, Bob. Move on.

If you fail to move on, more than your cost will be sunk.

An everyday example of Sunk Cost happened to me last month. I was on a cruise ship, and paid for an excursion to see the mansions in Newport, Rhode Island. When the time came to leave our ship I didn't want to go. I preferred to take a nap and do some writing. I stayed in my cabin.

Did I waste my money? I don't think so. I paid for an option to go on the excursion. The money was gone. Sunk Cost. The important question was: how could I best enjoy my afternoon? My answer is that I thoroughly enjoyed myself in my cabin. (I think Daveen thoroughly enjoyed her afternoon in our cabin too.)

Ask yourself what you would rather do today, not what you have already paid for.

Yesterday evening Daveen and I attended a musical I had been interested in seeing for several years. The tickets were expensive.

The seats were near the front of the auditorium. We disliked the hour-long first act and left at intermission. No sense throwing good time after bad.

Got it? Good. Sunk Cost. Let's practice Sunk Cost by going on to the next People Tool. Why spend any more time on this one?

GET PAST PERFECT

But men are men; the best sometimes forget.

—SHAKESPEARE
Othello

A man has but a certain strength; imperfections cling to him, which if he wait till he have brushed off entirely, he will spin forever on his axis, advancing nowhither."

—THOMAS CARLYLE
Letter to John Sterling [1835]

I used to be a partial perfectionist.

I say partial because certain aspects of my life, such as my clothing, weren't especially important to me and I didn't need them to be perfect. With my young children I decided that my enthusiasm and support were more important than my insisting on perfect crayon drawings in the first grade. I did hope, of course, that my family and I were on our way toward perfection in other areas, such as efficiency, since I like to move toward two or more goals at the same time.

I say perfectionist because often I would settle for nothing less than that ideal. In junior high school I wanted straight A's on my report card. In high school I wanted the highest grade in every class. When I began practicing law I wanted each letter or agreement to be perfectly composed and perfectly typed, and that was in the days before computers or word processing equipment made at least the typing relatively easy.

After a few years running my own law office I found that I was a hopeless prisoner of perfection. Some of the troubles I encountered in that particular trap were:

1. Perfection was costly. I was paying my secretary a lot of money to retype letters so they had absolutely no visible erasures.

2. My output was less than perfect because perfection took a lot of time. (I still hear a little voice inside my head saying, "Alan, don't lower your standards, don't lower your standards. Lowering your standards is a slippery slope.")

3. I was always dissatisfied with my own work and the work of everyone else in my office. This meant work wasn't much fun for them or for me.

4. I procrastinated. When I faced a new project, such as handling my first probate, I was afraid I wouldn't do it perfectly. So I put it off, in one case for more than a year, until my client dropped by to take the file to another attorney who would actually do the work, perhaps imperfectly.

5. I often fell short of my goal. I found that I couldn't be perfect—at least, not very often. I was disappointed in myself.

By age thirty I finally acknowledged what must have been perfectly obvious to everyone but me: though I aimed for perfection I almost always fell short. I was a failed perfectionist. Ouch!

A year or two later I realized even more fully that the quest for perfection carries a high price. I met Peter, a young man who was still a robust perfectionist. I had purchased an IBM 5110 computer for my property management business. At that time there was no suitable software for property management so I hired Peter to write a custom program. As a side benefit he would teach me how to program in Basic, an early computer language.

Peter began work in March. For months we worked together into the night, and I gradually learned a part of the theory and practice of computer programming. Peter was marvelous. Every week he invented a new shortcut or proposed an even more elegant algorithm. He even experimented with a rudimentary word processing program. Peter was a genius, and I was certain that eventually he would create a program that would be the envy of the industry.

Highlight "eventually." Spring passed into summer. Soon it was Thanksgiving and we seemed no closer to actually using the wonderful product of Peter's inspiration than we had been in March.

"Peter, when do you think you'll be finished? We're going to have to start using the computer in our business soon."

"Just a few more months. I'm working on some entirely new functions which will really speed up the processing time."

"Okay, but we really need to finish soon."

Peter programmed on. And on. Nights and weekends he haunted our office. I found him hunched over the miniature video screen at 7:00 a.m. Monday morning and at 11:00 p.m. Saturday night. Takeout bags from McDonald's littered his desk. Peter was a workaholic. Perfectionists often are. They have to be.

On December 15th I faced a decision. Either we would begin using our computer, which had now been sitting in our office for almost a year, on January 1st, or our accounting department would have to spend the next three weeks preparing manual records and forms for the new year. I talked to our extraordinary programmer.

"Peter, the computer goes live on January 1st."

"No way."

"We're going to do it."

"Alan, I don't see how. I've been doing some new research, and I think I can figure a way to make the program work for up to five thousand apartment units, and—"

"Peter, we only have two thousand apartments to account for."

"But I want to provide room for growth."

"Peter, we have to start using what you're working on. If we don't, I'm going to immediately have to start three people preparing manual records for next year. And if we don't start using the computer in January we're going to have a horrible mess trying to combine the first few months of manual records with computer accountings later in the year."

"I understand, but I want to make the program as good as it can possibly be. I need more time. Maybe by March 1st," he offered.

"January 1st. Not negotiable. If it's less than perfect, so be it. We're better off using what you can finish by January 1st than waiting for the perfect program you might have ready by sometime in the next century."

Peter sighed. "I'll see what I can do."

The following January 7th we went live on our new computer. The programming gods must have been smiling because the transition was surprisingly smooth. Our new program was certainly less than perfect, but it worked just fine and I was pleased that we had progressed past perfect.

A short time later I was involved in producing two feature length films. The glamorous part was the planning. Shooting the film was more of a chore and a bore than I could have possibly imagined. Postproduction—the editing, music, and sound effects—seemed to go on forever. I experienced firsthand the Hollywood saying that a motion picture is never completed. At some point you just have to give up and release it into the theaters.

Get Past Perfect.

When my daughter Heather was six she came into my library to visit, and showed me two of her drawings. "This is the fast drawing, and this is the slow drawing," she said.

"Is that because you drew one fast and one slow?" I asked.

"Yes."

I liked both. Heather liked to have fun, and was not concerned with perfection. As a result, I think she came closer to perfection than most of us. She didn't even need the 80% Solution.

I have nothing against perfection, especially when I'm at 37,000 feet in an airplane. But I know that my life is more fun, and more productive, when I use the tool and Get Past Perfect.

TAKE A CHANCE

And how am I to face the odds
Of man's bedevilment and God's?
I, a stranger and afraid
In a world I never made.

—A. E. HOUSEMAN
Last Poems

It is only by risking our persons from one hour to another that we live at all. And often enough our faith beforehand in an uncertified result is the only thing that makes the result come true.

—WILLIAM JAMES
from *The Will to Believe and Other Essays in Popular Philosophy*

On March 1, 1968, my law partner, Jim Hancock, and I formed a company to invest in real estate. I went out into the world and agreed to buy houses and apartment buildings, promising down payments of $5,000 or $25,000 in thirty or sixty days. There was just one small problem. Neither Jim nor I had the money to close an escrow. I always came up with the down payment, somehow, but those were scary times.

After two or three years of watching me repeatedly put our financial lives at the precipice, Jim cornered me in my office one afternoon and told me that he didn't like what I was doing.

"Jim," I said. "Between us we have a net worth of about $15,000. Suppose we take the risk, run our net worth up to $1,000,000 over the next few years then lose it all? We would have gone from almost nothing to really nothing. No huge loss. But suppose we run our net worth up to a million dollars and keep it? We could be set for the rest of our lives." Ah, youth, optimism, and inexperience!

Though Jim was polite, his fear continued to push him toward caution. This is one reason why, in 1971, Jim left our firm to practice law with different—and I assume more financially conservative—partners. I continued to take those same scary financial risks. It was a "bet" that I eventually won. And I found there is no substitute for long hours, experience, and a little bit of luck.

With women, however, I was more like Jim with money. Even as a high school student taking dance lessons, I could only gather enough courage to ask a girl to dance with me when she was waltzing off on the arm of some other guy. I was paralyzed by my fear of rejection, so I didn't get to practice my fox trot with very many girls.

With my body, to this day I refuse to take much risk. You won't find me climbing Mount Everest or playing ice hockey. I don't like pain, and I prefer to avoid even a remote possibility of my accidental death. As a result, I have denied myself the thrill of physical triumph. I will never stand on the top of a major mountain, unless it is a short and safe walk from my parked car.

I've noticed, however, as I'm sure you have, that where we take the greatest risks we reap the greatest reward. In fact, isn't that the only way to achieve a great reward? You may believe that when you take great risk you also risk great loss, but I say that the "great risk" is often an illusion. Here's why.

At high school dance after high school dance I doomed myself to failure for just one reason—I refused to try. No ask (no risk), no dance. No dance, no date. No date, no . . . you get the picture. Suppose I had been more assertive? Even today I partly cringe at the thought of risking my sacred self-esteem, but would I have really suffered 100 percent rejection? Not likely. Would I have enjoyed the pleasure of whirling around the dance floor holding a girl in my arms? Yes. So by "taking a chance" I would have gained more and lost less, other than a little temporary self-esteem. And I would have gained experience to help me in the future. As the poet John Dryden said, "None but the brave deserves the fair," (Alexander's Feast 1697).

On a deep level we all fear rejection. I know that I do. But my fear of loss is not the same as loss itself. A few years ago, at age sixty, my younger brother died of a sudden heart attack. I had always assumed that both of us would survive well into old age. I had no fear of losing David, but I lost him anyway. I'll say it again—the fear of loss is not the same as loss itself. It is not loss itself which deters us, it is the fear of loss. And as Franklin Delano Roosevelt reminded us, "The only thing we have to fear is fear itself" (First Inaugural Address, March 4, 1933).

I encourage you to use this tool: Take a Chance. Not blindly, not stupidly, but deliberately and more often than you do now. It is important to remember that it is often better to enjoy seven victories and three losses than to experience only a single victory.

When I say "not stupidly" I suggest that you find areas, such as the dance floor, where the real risk is slight even when the imaginary risk is great. The same principle applies in many other areas.

This is why I propose that you take a close, rational look at those areas in your life in which you would like "more." More money, more friends, more travel, more anything. Next you need to identify the specifics about what the risks really are, as compared with the possible rewards. Look for areas, such as politely asking for a slightly higher increase in salary, where the real risk is a lot lower than the perceived risk. Then go for it!

You may find that there are some areas—for me, my physical safety—in which the loss could be catastrophic and you do not want to take any risk at all. That's perfectly fine. We will never meet at the top of Mount Kilimanjaro. But we might share a real estate investment. Or a dance.

PEOPLE
18
TOOL

THE SIZZLE AND THE STEAK

It is the sizzle that sells the steak and not the cow ...
—ELMER WHEELER
Principle Number 1 of Salesmanship

Some enchanted evening ...
You may see a stranger
Across a crowded room.
—OSCAR HAMMERSTEIN II
South Pacific

One enchanted afternoon, I met my wife through the corner of my eye. As a customer in a rare bookstore, and as I walked past bookshelves filled with first editions, I almost didn't notice her at work behind a desk at the other end of the room.

"Yes!" a voice screamed inside my head. "This woman is for you!"

At that moment I didn't know if she was married (she wasn't). I didn't know if she had a sense of humor (she did). I didn't even know what she really looked like, since I was talking to the rare book dealer and he was trying to sell me something, so I was distracted. In short, I had no idea who this woman was. I only knew I loved her and believed in love at first sight. I fell in love with the sizzle. I knew very little about the steak.

We often make major life decisions based on scant information. To do this we use symbolism, a valuable human shortcut. This process of acting on the sizzle is unavoidable, usually appropriate, and often crucial to our well-being. Many, if not most, of our actions are based upon symbols. That's why the sizzle, and not the cow, sells the steak. The sizzle sounds and smells like something good to eat. The cow evokes an image of milk and manure. (Of course, for non-meat eaters, even the sizzle of the steak may have no allure.)

I still remember watching the first Nixon-Kennedy debate on television. I was sure that JFK won. So were most people who watched the debate on TV. Nixon sported a five o'clock shadow and looked pale. But most people who listened to the debate on the radio thought it was even. Appearance was the sizzle, not the words.

Suppose you are lost in a foreign city and three complete strangers walk toward you. The first is a man with a three-day growth of beard. The second is a young woman pushing a baby in a stroller. The third is wearing a uniform. Which one will you approach to ask for help?

Unavoidably, your answer will depend upon your own personal symbolism. I would try either the young woman ("safe") or the uniform ("authoritative"). I would avoid the scruffy man ("dangerous").

I do not claim that I would make the best decision, but my choice, or yours, in this situation must be based entirely upon our respective personal symbolism, and not upon complete information. The unkempt man could be friendly and knowledgeable. The uniformed person might be ignorant or treacherous. The young woman could be reluctant to talk with a stranger. But, right or wrong, we act on the assumption that our symbols accurately represent the real thing.

Back at the rare bookstore many years ago did I love my future wife because she reminded me of my mother? Because of the way she tilted her head? Because she seemed so involved in what she was doing? Yes to all of these symbols. I used my imagination to flesh her out from the limited information I had observed. I sensed that I "knew" her even though, of course, I did not.

Be consciously aware of your personal symbols.

Think of someone you know fairly well—your spouse, parent, or a friend. Would his or her reaction to various symbols be exactly the same as yours? Of course not. Each of us is different, yet we often assume that our own personal symbolism is universal.

I believe in love at first sight. How could you possibly not?

How can anyone associate the word "computer" with "fear and loathing," when it says to me "productivity and fun"?

When you buy a car, are you buying metal and glass, or the design or hood ornament?

Do you only date men who are more than six feet tall?

Have you voted the straight Democratic (or Republican) ticket for your entire life? If your symbol of "Republican" or "Democrat" goes back to the days of Dwight D. Eisenhower and Adlai Stevenson, or even John F. Kennedy and Richard Nixon, take another look. Your symbolism might be out of date.

Symbols are a useful shortcut. They can tell you who is worth pursuing across a crowded room. They can suggest which food you might enjoy. But remember to remain consciously aware of your symbols and to often peer through or beyond them.

In building the life of your dreams you may marry a complex, surprising human being, who is more than just a gorgeous body, a Catholic, or a CPA. The stuff of your life is more than just an enticing sizzle or advertising promise. The sizzle is not the steak. But it is the sizzle, which we must recognize for what it is.

PEOPLE
19
TOOL

BLIND DATE—MAKE A GOOD FIRST IMPRESSION

A journey of a thousand miles must begin with a single step.
—LAO-TZU
The Way of Lao-Tzu, #64

And the evening and the morning were the first day.
—THE BIBLE
The First Book of Moses

A number of years ago Gina, a good friend and investor of mine, referred a woman friend of hers to me to discuss a real estate investment which I had available. Her friend appeared at my offices at the appointed time, together with her financial advisor who had offices in Century City, an upscale high-rise office complex next to Beverly Hills.

The three of us spent a pleasant hour and a half together. I explained the virtues and vices of investing with me and the prospective investor asked a number of questions as did her financial advisor. When they left I doubted she would invest with me, because folks with financial advisors seldom do. In my experience financial advisors prefer to profit by selling their clients the financial advisor's investments.

I was not prepared, however, for the peculiar reaction which came to light a few days later when Gina called me.

"Is everything OK with you?" she asked.

"Yes, as far as I know. Anything specific?"

"Financially. Are you OK financially?

"I think so. Same as always. A little better all the time. Why do you ask?"

"Well, my friend was concerned. She's not going to invest with you because your offices . . . well, she thought that your offices were shabby."

I smiled. "Gina, as you know, I don't believe in high overhead. We own our own building, and I certainly haven't spent a lot of money to make it impressive. It's a working office."

"I know, and my friend wasn't impressed."

"Gina, as always, I appreciate the referral, and I entirely respect your friend's decision."

So on this blind date with a prospective investor I made a bad first impression because my office was not extraordinary and I suppose that my desk, as usual, evidenced a disordered mind (I'm not very good at organizing things physically). I lost a potential sale.

I will also report that three years later Gina called me again.

"Remember the friend I referred to you three years ago—the one with the financial advisor?

"Of course I do." Very few prospective investors fail to invest with me, and I remember those failures as I always want to improve.

"Well, Alan, now she's really not going to invest with you."

"Darn! Do my offices look worse now than they did three years ago?"

"No. She invested everything with her financial advisor and he lost it all."

I couldn't resist smiling. Appearance isn't everything, but it is part of the sizzle, and it does help to make a good first impression. I'm sure the financial advisor rented much nicer office space than mine.

In 1969 I was a student in a class on personality at the University of Southern California, taught by a PhD in psychology. He mentioned that when he was in graduate school he and two of his classmates became close friends. There was a fourth student who wanted to be part of their group, but he seemed like a nerd so they excluded him.

"By the third year," my professor said, "he seemed to be a pretty nice guy, but we still excluded him. First impressions endure."

There is a hamburger restaurant on 6th Street in Los Angeles where I eat lunch every time I'm in the area. Their hamburgers and potato salad are outstanding. Years ago they opened a branch in Encino, which is much closer to my office. A week after they opened I made it a point to arrive for lunch. The man ahead of me at the cashier was with a party of fifteen or twenty friends, and he was complaining that two of their orders had not been filled. I believe that the cashier was also the manager, and a relative of the owner of the 6th Street store.

To my dismay, the cashier was nasty with the customer ahead of me.

I was brash in those days, and as I paid I said to the cashier/ manager, "I don't think you're going to encourage business here by treating your customers rudely."

His response was entirely in character, and entirely unexpected.

"People come here for the food. He'll come back if he likes the food." The cashier slammed my change down in front of me.

I never returned to the Encino store. I was not at all surprised when it closed less than a year later.

As they say, you only have one chance to make a good first impression.

PEOPLE **20** TOOL

MAKE LEMONADE

When the world serves you lemons, make lemonade.
—JEROME LAWRENCE and ROBERT E. LEE
Auntie Mame

There is nothing either good or bad, but thinking makes it so.
—WILLIAM SHAKESPEARE
Hamlet, Act II, Scene ii

I was talking to my close business associate Gary last week. We found ourselves complaining about one of our shopping centers, which has performed badly for more than a year despite our best efforts to turn it around. We decided to put it up for sale.

At the end of our conversation Gary asked, "How can you be so cheerful about a center which we might have to sell at a loss?"

"Because I've learned a great deal from this investment about what *not* to buy in the future." As I spoke I suddenly recognized a specific habit of thinking that I have unconsciously followed for years.

"Gary, no matter what comes along—something painful, something fun—I always ask myself, 'How can I put this information or experience to good use in my life?'"

When I was fourteen years old I went shopping one afternoon after school for a birthday gift for Cathy Ferris, who I hoped would be my girlfriend.

When I came home with Cathy's gift, about 6:30 p.m., I told my parents that I had a pain on my right side below my stomach. This kind of complaint was unusual for me, and my parents immediately called the doctor. They belonged to a medical plan, with doctors in those days who actually made house calls.

A short while later the doctor showed up, asked me to "lower my trousers," then pushed on my abdomen. He asked, "Does that hurt?"

"Ouch!"

"Does that hurt?" He pushed again.

"Ow! Stop!"

An hour later I was in a hospital for the first time in my life. They drew blood—ouch again—then a doctor came into the room.

"Your white blood cell count is high. You probably have appendicitis," he said.

Then he put on some white gloves—probably rubber in 1954—and proceeded with a rectal exam. This was new to me, but despite my strong protest he proceeded with his dirty deed. Then he left. Ten minutes later a second doctor showed up. When he began to pull on a fresh pair of white gloves I almost shouted, "The other doctor already did that."

"Yes," he said. "But I'm the surgeon. We're going to take out your appendix, and I have to know exactly where it is."

That stopped me, and at eleven o'clock that evening I was wheeled into an operating room. The anesthesiologist put a needle in a vein on the back of my hand and asked me to count backward from a hundred. I think I got to 97.

The operation was a success, but I was out of school the next day and the entire following week.

What has this story got to do with Making Lemonade? Because that is the first time I clearly remember using the tool of Making Lemonade. I had always tried to avoid physical pain, and here I was, suffering a whole lot of pain and there was absolutely nothing I could do about it other than have surgery and, perhaps, suffer even more pain until I recovered. Being practical, as I lay on that hospital bed in the examination room I decided to use the pain by remembering it for the rest of my life, and appreciating when pain was absent from my body in the future. With few lapses I have done exactly that, and Making Lemonade has served me well. I appreciate my relative good health more than I otherwise might have. I know my life is going to be over one day, and I might as well welcome every moment with as much enthusiasm as I can muster.

But there's more to lemonade than that. Most of us believe, accurately, that success breeds more success. A good student in high school is likely to be a good student in college. A movie director who wins an Oscar is likely to direct future successful films. An athlete who wins an Olympic gold medal is likely to be a winner in later competitions. (Patterns Persist.)

But isn't it equally true that failure can lead to success? A scientist will tell us that each failure is a success. One more possibility that doesn't work brings us closer to the still unknown possibility that will work. We need to remember that success does not spring full grown, as Minerva from the head of Jupiter. Every time I write—even an e-mail—I am unhappy with the result, not because it is particularly good or bad, but because I always expect my first draft to be perfect. This always goes badly for me, because I fail to realize that most good professional writing is the product of many drafts and editorial comments. So is my first draft a failure? Not at all. It is the foundation for a potential success.

Yes, a lemon tastes sour, which is not in and of itself a bad thing. But add a little sugar water and you have a drink which many love, especially on a hot summer's day.

And what of Cathy Ferris, the girl I had hoped would be my girlfriend so many years ago? She tragically committed suicide in her twenties. And I am still sad, very sad, that she didn't have the long and happy life which she might have, and that our friendship didn't deepen and flourish. Her suicide was and is, for me, as sour as a lemon gets. But my task is to squeeze that loss into the pitcher of my life, mix it with the wonderful memories of her which I do have, and, from time to time, many years later, enjoy—if you will—the sweetness mixed with the sour.

Trudy Goodman, a friend of mine who founded Insight LA, a mindfulness meditation center in Los Angeles, describes her last conversations with Maurine, who had been her teacher for more than ten years. Maurine was dying. Trudy writes:

"I decided to go for it—maybe it's my last chance to ask her what I most wanted to know. 'After a whole life of Zen practice, teaching, and deep enlightenment, what's the truest thing you can say to me now?'"

Maurine didn't miss a beat. Speaking with her usual authority and power, she said simply, "Live it up!"

Make Lemonade.

FRY ANOTHER EGG

*He that will not apply new remedies must expect new evils;
for time is the greatest innovator.*
—FRANCIS BACON
"Of Innovations," from Essays of Thomas Bacon

To know is nothing at all; to imagine is everything.
—ANATOLE FRANCE
The Crime of Sylvestre Bonnard

You do not always have to live with what makes you unhappy.

When it comes to breakfast I am a creature of habit. Years ago every morning I fried one "over easy" egg for myself. I liked the yolk medium, not hard. One morning, as I dropped the egg into the frying pan, the shell punctured the yolk, which broke. I frowned, and resigned myself to an unsatisfying breakfast because I knew that when I turned the egg over the yolk would become hard.

I glared at the offending egg. I tried to console myself by thinking about lunch. Then a thought popped into my head. "This egg costs about twenty cents. I can throw it away and cook another egg exactly the way I like it—'over easy.'"

So I did.

Often when I find a better way of doing something that I have done for years I ask myself, "Why didn't I think of that sooner?"

Well, I didn't, and one purpose of this book is to remind both of us that there is usually a better way of doing anything. We just haven't thought of it yet.

Recently my friend Gloria complained to me about her two-year-old sun-room floor. "The tile is pitting and the floor is ugly. It wasn't glazed properly in the first place. I really don't like it, but I guess I have to live with it," she said. Gloria probably meant for the rest of her life.

"Why not take the nice throw rug you have in your second bedroom, and put that over the tile?" I said. "It would look beautiful there,"

"The egg!" She remembered the story I had told her years before.

"Exactly. The egg. You don't have to live with a floor you really don't like."

Together, we moved the rug to its new home. When the yolk breaks, I Fry Another Egg.

THE FOUR C'S

It's always too early to quit.

—NORMAN VINCENT PEALE

Extreme fear can neither fight nor fly.

—WILLIAM SHAKESPEARE
King Richard III

Years ago I saw a play three times in one week. It was written and directed by my friend David Beaird. I have forgotten the title, but I remember the essence: to solve a difficult and urgent problem use the "Four C's."

OK. What are the "Four C's"?

Imagine that you're flying in an airplane and are lost. If you don't solve the problem you will die. What to do, what to do?

The first C is Confess. Confess that you are lost. It's like alcoholism, or a miserable marriage. You have to first admit that you have a problem that you need to solve. Although this seems obvious, most of us prefer the comfort of feeling that we are in control of the situation. That can be a mistake, sometimes a big mistake. At age sixty-five my mother discovered a lump in her right breast. She didn't tell anyone for ten months. That turned out to be a very bad idea.

The second C is Climb. Climb as high as you can, both to give yourself more time to solve the problem and to open yourself to a broader perspective. By climbing higher you might see an airport.

Or a thunderstorm chasing you. Perhaps another airplane. You want to access as much information as you can.

The third C is Contact. Contact a ground station. Ask for help. "Houston, we have a problem." You have to publically admit that you need help. That step is difficult for many of us, unless we are in serious pain. To paraphrase Proust, "We listen to pleasure. We obey pain." Isn't it better to solve the problem before you double up and become immobilized? A close friend of mine was experiencing financial problems. She was having difficulty making her mortgage payments and fell further and further behind. When she finally made an appointment with a financial advisor she was in serious jeopardy of losing her home. Jim Henson, fifty-three years old, creator of *The Muppets*, died of organ failure because of a strep infection. Quick action could have saved him. He didn't want to be a bother to people, and refused to go to the hospital.

The fourth C is Commit. Commit to a course of action. You might have limited time before your airplane runs out of fuel. Then the engine will stop and your airplane will crash—with you in it. You have to do something. You have time for only one maneuver. It's like the Aesop's fable of "The Cat and the Fox." One day the hunting dogs began to chase both a cat and a fox. The cat immediately climbed up a tree to safety. The fox used many strategies: double back and forth, run through a stream to throw the dogs off his scent, hide in a burrow. Nothing worked for the fox (no relation to me), who was eventually caught. Moral of the story: one trick, when it works, is better than many. So commit to your course of action—it's time to perform.

There it is. Memorize the Four C's. Or write them down on a notepad or on your electronic device. And think about the situations in which you can use the Four C's. When you need them it may be too late to look them up.

Confess.
Climb.
Contact.
Commit.

STUFF IT INTO YOUR SUB

The great decisions of human life have as a rule far more to do with the instincts and other mysterious unconscious factors than with conscious will and well-meaning reasonableness. The shoe that fits one person pinches another; there is no recipe for living that suits all cases.
—CARL GUSTAV JUNG
Modern Man in Search of a Soul

He who knows others is wise;
He who knows himself is enlightened.
—LAO-TZU
The Way of Lao-Tzu

When I was a freshman in college I came across one paragraph in my Psych 101 textbook which presented an idea I have used with outstanding success ever since. I have to admit that in college my primary goal was not to learn anything. I just wanted to get the best grades I could. Yes, I was lazy. I still am, though Daveen says I should consider myself to be "efficient," which sounds better. But I must have learned something along the way, not by mastering entire books, but rather by remembering and using those ideas which seemed useful to me. This was one of the best.

Simply put, the idea I found in Psych 101 was that your subconscious (your "sub" for purposes of this chapter) can solve a problem for you without active conscious effort. If you need to solve a problem but can't come up with an immediate answer, all you have to do is stuff the information and the problem into your sub. Then revisit your sub in an hour or day or week and see if your sub has finished its work. While this is not an infallible solution, it certainly helps me most of the time.

Originally the idea appealed to me because it was easy. I didn't have to think. It was like sending my car through a car wash which would automatically clean it. Of course, the sub is even better than a car wash because it deals with big problems, and—best of all—it doesn't cost a dime.

My wife asks me to drive from Los Angeles to San Francisco to see our daughter Ingrid present her final report in a college class. I want to please Daveen and I want to support Ingrid. But I don't like driving eleven hours round trip, and I'm not sure I can afford to take a full day and a half away from work. When you're lazy deadlines seem to often catch up with you. So I stuffed the problem into my sub. Solution: Daveen drove up and back because she wanted to deliver a carful of something to Ingrid. I flew both ways.

In writing this book I've paid close attention to how I solve challenges in my life. When my process is clear but the name of the tool is not I simply stuffed the People Tool into my sub, which has given me many chapter titles that I have used.

To be efficient, and solve a problem which baffles your conscious mind, just Stuff It into Your Sub.

SMILEY FACE

What's the use of worrying?
It never was worthwhile,
So, pack up your troubles in your old kit-bag,
And smile, smile, smile.

—GEORGE ASAF (GEORGE H. POWELL)
"Pack Up Your Troubles in Your Old Kit-Bag"

Peace begins with a smile.
—MOTHER TERESA

For twenty years I had a smiley face printed on my personal checks. People who received those checks asked me, "Why is there a smiley face on your check? Writing a check means that you're spending money, and no one likes to spend money."

Not me. My thought in having a smiley face printed on each of my personal checks was simple. I was happy to write the check and pay money to someone else because whatever they gave me in return made me happier than keeping the money. If I was more content with the money in my bank account I would not have written the check. Too bad my present bank doesn't offer a smiley face, but banks today may have less of a sense of humor.

My point is that we make decisions all the time, then act on those decisions. Whatever the decision, Smiley Face says that we should, as the old song goes, accentuate the positive, eliminate the negative.

Often the choice is absolutely clear. If you need to use either a bus or your car you will have to do a little walking. Smile while you walk. Enjoy yourself. Why grumble? Even if your knee hurts, you could be in a wheelchair.

Often a choice is not completely clear. Should you get a flu shot this year? The shot may hurt, it may even make you mildly sick, and you may have to pay for it. All negatives. But if you don't get the flu shot you may get the flu.

You can decide to get the flu shot, or not. Whatever you decide, use Smiley Face, which is a subsidiary of Make Lemonade. And my son Craig tells me that research indicates that smiling, all by itself, can improve your mood.

Think about it. And smile while you do.

PEOPLE 25 TOOL

SHOWBIZ

Leave 'em wanting more.
—SHOW BUSINESS ADAGE

Nothing recedes like excess.
—ALAN FOX

When I was twelve years old my mother took my younger brother and me to Hawaii to meet my father who had been traveling in Asia with the Xavier Cugat band. We stayed for a week at a small motel in Waikiki. By now a fifty story hotel has undoubtedly risen from the same plot of land.

In Honolulu we toured the Dole pineapple plant where I celebrated Christmas in April. Pineapple. The sight of it. The scent of it. The taste of it, in unlimited quantities. And it was all free.

At the end of the tour there were water fountains from which no water flowed, just pineapple juice. Not from a can that cost eighteen cents, but from a pineapple juice fountain. And there was free pineapple as well. This was a once in a lifetime opportunity for a ravenous twelve-year-old boy. I ate pineapple. I drank pineapple. I practically bathed in pineapple juice.

You may be ahead of me. For the next year or more I could not stand the sight or taste of pineapple. And the thought of pineapple juice turned my stomach. At Dole I simply had too much.

And that is why, in show biz, you really do want to leave your audience wanting more. If you think they will sit still for twenty songs, sing fifteen. If they want three hours, give them two and a half. After all, you would like them to come back to see your next show.

I've applied the Dole lesson ever since, to myself. If I think I want ten days of vacation, I take eight. I eat at my favorite restaurant less often than I think I would prefer. I don't watch football on television twenty-four hours a day. Why ruin a good thing?

And why ruin a good thing for yourself? If you would like to have lunch with me twice a week, let's make it once. When my children were young I didn't buy them candy every time we went to the market. When you are tempted to overindulge in something you enjoy, think of Showbiz. In the interest of your own future enjoyment, you might leave yourself wanting more. And you might leave others wanting a little more as well.

Years ago, at the very end of a three day retreat, I asked a Texan who attended, "How did you like it?"

"Waahl," he drawled, "Ah feel like the monkey who made love to the skunk."

He paused for dramatic effect, then continued,

"Ah enjoyed about as much as Ah could stand."

Showbiz. In moderation, of course.

PEOPLE 26 TOOL

ERASE

... And when you gaze long into an abyss,
the abyss also gazes into you.

—FRIEDRICH WILHELM NIETZSCHE
Beyond Good and Evil

For each ecstatic instant
We must an anguish pay
In keen and quivering ratio
To the ecstasy.

—EMILY DICKENSON
No. 125 [c. 1859], stanza 1

There are times when a good memory is distinctly unhelpful. An example is my vacation in Antarctica almost five years ago.

I had made plans, chartered a ship, and invited family and friends in early 2008, almost a year in advance. On September 15, 2008, the world-wide investment firm Lehman Brothers filed for bankruptcy. What followed is either The Great Recession if you kept your job and home, or The Second Great Depression if you lost your job or your home. In any event, my business promptly went south, meaning that it began to lose large amounts of money instead of doing what I think it always should do—operate at a profit.

At any rate, I had made a large nonrefundable deposit for the ship charter and decided to make the trip despite the additional, but smaller, cost. That two-week trip was the best vacation of my life.

A large part of the reason why I enjoyed fourteen straight days of pleasure was that I erased the cost from my mind. Of course, it's like erasing a file on your computer; the file isn't really gone, just the pointers to it. So I did, briefly, remember the cost from time to time, but not for long and always together with the theory of sunk cost (money already spent is gone, focus instead on today and the future).

My larger point is this. We all make decisions every day, if only whether to get out of bed in the first place, or what to eat for breakfast. Virtually every alternative (stay in bed vs. get up; yogurt or eggs for breakfast) has advantages and disadvantages. If you stay in bed all day you might have to catch up on more work tomorrow. Eggs might taste better to you than light yogurt, but come with more calories. There is nothing you can do in life without cost, if only the cost of your time, and without forgoing alternatives.

But you will decide. Yes, I will get out of bed this morning. I will wear my favorite jeans (which, of course, over time will wear them out). This is why I want to enjoy each "ecstatic instant" and not "an anguish pay" (Emily Dickinson). I will make decisions and I will take action. So I use Erase, as much as I can, to reduce or at least confine my thoughts and uncomfortable feelings about the cost or lost alternatives. I also magnify the positives to maximize my enjoyment of the breakfast, the jeans, the view—whatever.

To Erase effectively you will need constant practice. Today is Father's Day, and I have been invited to my older son's house for a barbeque. But I have promised my publisher that I will turn in the revised and completed manuscript for People Tools tonight. I'm only halfway through, and the thought "I don't want to work all day on this" keeps taking me from my computer into the kitchen for a snack.

No more snacks. Erase that idea!

I'm sure that you can think of many examples in your own life where Erase will be helpful, and add to your enjoyment of every experience, every single day.

Erase does take practice. I'm still practicing, but with a Smiley Face.

THINGS ARE ONLY THINGS

And love can come to everyone,
The best things in life are free.
—Buddy De Sylva
"The Best Things in Life are Free" from *Good News*

I reserve my emotional energy
exclusively for people.
Things can be fixed.
Things can be replaced.
People cannot.
—Alan C. Fox

When I was eighteen I took the thousand-dollar inheritance from my grandmother, added my own savings of about seven hundred dollars, and bought my first car—a brand new metallic blue VW Bug. I picked it up in Costa Mesa, where I had found the best price, about sixty miles from my home. This was the first time I had ever driven a stick shift for any distance and I was very disappointed to find that my new VW was even more sluggish than its reputation. It wasn't until the next day that I realized I had driven my new car home with its emergency brake on. Ah, well. Even us old, wise folks were young once.

Since my father always parked his car in the garage, I parked mine on the street. A few weeks after my sluggish drive, as I walked toward my beautiful new car, my jaw dropped. I saw that my new

VW had been sideswiped, leaving two black scratches on its left rear fender. I was furious. My brand new car was ruined. I was enraged for a full month.

Finally, I realized that I had allowed my life to be ruined by my anger about those two ugly scratches, which might have been repaired for a few hundred dollars. But that was a lot of money to me in those days, and I never did have those scratches removed. Instead, I thought of something far better.

After a month of seething I realized that my anger wasn't doing me a bit of good. It couldn't help me to find or punish the culprit. It couldn't transform my car back to its original pristine condition. So I decided to let go of my anger, and for the rest of my life to never be upset about things. And a car, no matter how expensive or how beautiful, is only a thing. In my life I resolved to reserve my emotional energy exclusively for people. Things can be fixed. Things can be replaced. People cannot.

And I am pleased to report that from that day to this I have lived by my decision. I have not darkened my mood or my life with anger or regret about a thing.

The van I now own needs some bodywork. I refuse to be angry. I will just pay to have it fixed. When she was seventeen one of my daughters was diagnosed with type one diabetes. As I write this, her condition can be treated but it cannot be fixed. I worry about her, not the van.

I once traveled with my family to Australia where more than 95 percent of gem-quality opals are mined. One afternoon in Sydney, after a boat tour of its beautiful harbor, we stopped in a shop which our guide said was the best in Australia for buying opals. We were shown a brief movie about opal mining, peeked into their safe at what was presented as the most expensive opal in the world, and began to shop.

My wife collects rings. By now she probably would have one ring for each finger even if she had ten hands. I must admit that the opal ring she picked out in Sydney was drop-dead gorgeous. It was also drop-dead expensive, and probably cost as much as half of the other rings in her collection combined. We negotiated a 20 percent discount and a refund of the 11 percent tax when we left the country, and I reminded myself that an Australian dollar was equal to about seventy-eight cents American. So, with brief hesitation, I bought Daveen a beautiful and costly opal ring in Australia.

Although she seems to wear different rings every day, Daveen wore her green and blue opal every day for two weeks after we returned. Until we went to the theater.

When the curtain fell and the lights rose after the first act of *Dirty Rotten Scoundrels*, a musical playing at the Pantages Theater in Hollywood, Daveen gasped.

"My ring!"

I looked at her hand, and saw the thin gold outline of a ring, but no gemstone.

"Your orange stone?" I asked.

"No! My opal!"

Daveen doesn't panic easily and I'm not saying that she panicked then, but I was reminded about how I felt when I first saw those ugly scratches on my VW Bug.

We searched the floor. We searched the seats. Five ushers helped us during intermission. No opal.

Before the second act began Daveen ran to the lobby where she had previously bought a bottle of water. She didn't return until the show was over.

"It wasn't at the counter, it wasn't in the car, it wasn't on the sidewalk between the theater and the car." So after the show we searched the theater again, this time with eight or ten ushers helping out. No opal.

I certainly don't like to lose anything. Even more, I don't like someone else to lose a gift which I've given to them. Especially when the gift was expensive. But gone is gone and I refuse to be upset about the loss or destruction of a thing. So we gave our name and telephone number to the manager of the theater and left for home.

The drive, with another couple in the back seat, was silent. After we dropped them off we searched the street where we had picked them up. Nothing.

I thought that we had seen the last of the best opal I had ever owned, but I am pleased to report that the disaster of losing the (costly) gem did not spoil the rest of our night. Daveen, to her credit, seemed to put anguish aside, and we enjoyed our usual late night rituals.

This morning, before I left for my office, we talked about other things. Life went on, the new day would not be marred by a missing thing.

We each used the People Tool which I am writing about in this chapter: Things Are Only Things.

Do you like happy endings? I do.

I called Daveen.

"Hi, Daveen."

"Hi."

"I found the opal."

"Really?

"It was on my desk. It probably fell out when you picked me up at the office last night, and the cleaning crew must have found it and put it on my desk."

Silence. Then, "Thank goodness."

I love Daveen. I like, but do not love, any ring, no matter how expensive or how beautiful.

SWEET GRAPES

In the life of each of us, I said to myself, there is a place remote and islanded, and given to endless regret or secret happiness.

—SARAH ORNE JEWETT
The Country of the Pointed Firs

A hungry fox crept into a vineyard where bunches of ripe grapes dangled from high arbors. The fox leaped many times in his effort to win a juicy feast but failed every time. Finally he retreated in defeat, muttering to himself, "Well, what does it matter anyway? The grapes are sour."

—AESOP
The Fox and the Grapes

"Who needs that job, anyway?"

"He's such a nerd. I'm glad he didn't notice me!"

"Anyone who wins the lottery is going to waste all the money and end up worse off than before he bought the ticket."

Do any of the above "sour grapes" statements sound familiar to you?

Why not sweeten those grapes, and fully enjoy the delicious fruit within your grasp?

"I love my job. The hours are great, I feel productive, have good friends there, even though the pay is a little less than I think I'm worth."

"I'm lucky to have such a good friend as you."

"When I lost $500 in Las Vegas last week I had such a good time it was worth it."

When you make a decision you weigh the pros and cons. You may modify your options, but ultimately you have to say "Yes" or "No," and then you follow up with action.

I suggest that once you have decided, and especially when you are acting upon your decision ("Yes" or "No") you magnify the positives and minimize the negatives by looking at them through the wrong end of the telescope.

In short, when you decide, then act and, for example, attend a movie to please your family or your date, you may have mixed feelings. Forget that. If you are going to be at the movie anyway, why not put your emotional magnifying glass directly over the fantasy of the movie or the excitement of those with you, and even your grumpiness in being there. (Doesn't everyone enjoy complaining?)

My son the psychologist might call this rationalization. I call it tasting the sweetness in life.

Grapes. How sweet they are.

PEOPLE
29
TOOL

PARALLEL PATHS

Never judge a person until you have walked
for thirty days in his moccasins.
—NATIVE AMERICAN PROVERB

I cling to my own innards.
—ZELDA FITZGERALD

Would you be surprised to hear a five-year-old child speaking fluent Greek? Not if you are Greek and the child is Greek. In fact, I would be surprised to hear a Greek toddler living in Athens speaking fluent English.

How does a child learn to speak a "foreign" language? Simply by listening to others, and mimicking them. That's how we learn much of what we know. We observe others and model our speech and actions after theirs. For better or for worse, we copy most of the behavior that our role models use. That is why language, culture, and politics often run in the family.

It is important to my wife that she knows in advance when someone will arrive at our home. I don't care who shows up or when, but I don't like to be abandoned so I need to know when someone is leaving. There is no "right" or "wrong" here. There is only a difference.

To me, "please" and "thank you" are important. To Daveen, not quite so much. This is something else we feel differently about.

There is a sad but funny scene in the movie *Annie Hall*. Woody Allen and Diane Keaton are shown on opposite sides of a split screen while each one is in a therapy session. The two therapists ask their clients how often they make love.

"Hardly ever," says Woody Allen. "Maybe three times a week."

"Constantly," says Diane Keaton. "I'd say three times a week."

Again there is no "right" or "wrong," it is just a part of life that people view differently.

I prefer communicating in writing, which is why I receive and answer more than two hundred e-mails on most business days. My wife is verbal—she usually needs to recharge her cell phone battery in the afternoon.

In high school my niece Susie went out for gymnastics, though her father wanted her to choose a team sport such as baseball. She didn't like team sports but enjoyed gymnastics and was able to excel.

A friend of mine, Hugo, married a woman named Lauren. They moved into their home more than twenty years ago. She put all of her possessions in place within three days. Hugo still has boxes in the garage.

Finally, we all have fears. I am terrified of high places such as cliffs but I have never been afraid of money. Years ago the idea struck me that many people climb mountains and are not afraid of cliffs, while others have great fear around money and won't even talk about it. In an instant I realized that my fears are personal to me, and yours are personal to you. Our routes may be similar but they are not the same. We walk Parallel Paths.

Each of us truly is unique. And while you and I may both speak the same language, we certainly have a different vocabulary. You know words which I have never heard of, and I've read books which you may have never seen. We each have had different life experiences and, to paraphrase the words of Zelda Fitzgerald, we each cling to our own innards.

If you have ever traveled in a foreign country, you have heard a tourist, perhaps yourself, speaking English, very loudly. You think that if you speak loud enough, an Italian will understand you. But no. He or she has had a different life experience. English might be Greek to him or her. And we also may lead different lives because our culture is different, or our gender.

Our paths are not identical. This means that in every human interaction, you can't assume that the other person is just like you. Each of us has to learn to recognize, respect, and hopefully enjoy our differences. Our relationships with our partners, our children, and our friends are more satisfying and successful when we do. I raised my children differently than they raise my grandchildren. Though we all live on the same planet, we cannot walk precisely in each other's footsteps.

We tread Parallel Paths.

CATCH THEM BEING GOOD

One must separate from anything that forces one to repeat No again and again.

—FRIEDRICH WILHELM NIETZSCHE
Ecce Homo

Catch them being good.

—WESLEY BECKER
Parents Are Teachers

I was sitting in class at the University of Southern California a number of years ago learning about psychology.

"The strongest reinforcement of behavior," the professor said, "is positive reinforcement. If you want someone to repeat a behavior, give them praise. Negative reinforcement, criticism for mistakes, is not as effective. If you want to extinguish a behavior, it's best to simply ignore it."

I was astonished. I couldn't believe that an experienced professor at a major university could make such an elementary mistake.

"I think you got that backwards, sir," I blurted out.

Every eye focused on me.

"What do you mean?" he asked.

"It's simple. Everyone knows that the best way to get people, especially children, to change their behavior is to correct their mistakes and to punish them, if necessary."

Several heads nodded in agreement. Encouraged, I pushed on.

"And if you praise someone, they'll be satisfied and stop doing whatever it is they did to earn your approval in the first place."

The professor smiled. "You're absolutely certain of this, Mr. Fox?"

"Yes, I am. That's what my father did. He always let me know when I was wrong. That's what I've always done."

"Are you willing to try an experiment, to test your hypothesis, so to speak?"

"Sure."

"Good," he said. "That's very good. I admire your search for truth."

"Thank you." I felt vindicated already.

"During the coming week, I'd like you to 'catch them being good.'"

"Yes?"

He just smiled.

"What else?"

"Nothing else. When you find anyone, including yourself, per-forming a behavior that you would like them to repeat, simply say, 'That's great. I really like that.'"

"'That's great, I really like that'?"

"Exactly. Very good."

"Then what, professor?"

He looked surprised. "Then? Make a record of what happens with the behavior you praise. See how many times it's repeated."

"It won't be repeated."

"Ah," he said, "isn't that exactly what you're setting out to discover?"

"Yes, sir." I couldn't wait to prove him wrong.

At home that evening my wife fixed my favorite dinner, sweet and sour meatballs. She did this maybe once every six months. Nor-mally, I would have said something funny like, "It's about time you made sweet and sour meatballs again," but tonight I was a scientist.

"Wow! Darling, this is my favorite dinner in the whole world. Thank you. I appreciate your going to the trouble."

She was obviously surprised, since my enthusiasm was entirely out of character. She smiled through her confusion.

"Thank you." Then she kissed me.

"I like that, too." Sometimes the pursuit of scientific truth requires sacrifice.

When she kissed me again, I was too pleased to realize that her second kiss might point to a flaw in my theory.

Then I heard my son, Steve, practicing the accordion. My father was a professional musician, and I had been taught to be a critical listener. A very critical listener. I once attended a recital by the renowned pianist, Vladimir Horowitz, and found his performance to be only slightly above my minimum standard. Six-year-old Steve had a long way to go.

Nevertheless, I wandered into the living room where he was vigorously pushing and pulling the bellows of his bulky instrument.

When he finished a tune I could barely recognize as "Happy Birthday," I said, "Steve, you're making excellent progress."

He looked up at me, glowing. "Thanks, Dad. Would you like to hear 'Home on the Range'? That's a tough one."

"Sure, Steve." As he struggled on I remembered how I had felt when I was six, practicing the piano. My father didn't ignore me. He helped me to improve by pointing out every mistake. Could that be why I had practiced as little as I could get away with?

"Well, Dad, what do you think?"

What I thought was . . . that I should catch Steve being good.

"You're putting in a lot of practice on that song."

"Yes. It's the one I chose for the recital."

"I like hearing you practice. I'll bet you're going to be wonderful at the recital."

"Thanks, Dad. It's a lot more fun to practice when you listen to me."

Now it was my turn to smile. "Good, Steve. That's good."

When I walked through the front door, I had intended to read the newspaper. Now I changed my mind and listened to the rest of his practice. I began to wonder if Steve knew something about psychology that I had yet to learn. Was he in cahoots with my professor?

The following week the psychology professor turned to me expectantly.

"Well, Mr. Fox. Will you share with us the result of your experiment?"

I cleared my throat. "Pretty interesting, sir. Three dinners of sweet-sour meatballs and a fairly good rendition of 'Home on the Range' by my six-year-old son. And countless kisses from my wife."

The class laughed.

"I'm relieved," the professor said. "Apparently you have replicated the result other researchers have demonstrated. I'm glad the world remains safe for psychology. I'm sure you're going to be very good at it."

"Thank you, sir." I couldn't resist adding, "I know what you're doing, sir. And it's working."

Over the following months, I tried to catch everyone I knew being good. I became less and less surprised, and more and more delighted, to find that everyone seemed to find my praise encouraging.

I have even learned to enjoy catching myself being good. It's fun.

A LITTLE BIT OF OIL

Everything is soothed by oil, and this is the reason why divers send out small quantities of it from their mouths, because it smoothes every part which is rough.
—PLINY THE ELDER
Natural History

Woe to him who seeks to pour oil upon the waters when God has brewed them into a gale! Woe to him who seeks to please rather than to appall!
—HERMAN MELVILLE
Moby Dick

As a boy I spent countless nights with my flashlight, reading science fiction in bed under my covers. I was fourteen when I read the short story "A Little Bit of Oil."

The setting was a spaceship conducting man's third ten-year expedition to the nearest star. The first two voyages had failed when the four-person crew neared Earth. Each spacecraft had mysteriously disappeared, never to be heard from again.

This third try was different. One crewmember was an enigma. He prepared the meals and entertained the pilot, copilot, and science officer throughout the trip, but when he tried to help it was clear he had no experience either as a scientist or pilot. The other three crewmembers more and more saw him as a misfit, especially when, dressed in a clown costume, he made them laugh.

On this third trip, as the spaceship reentered the solar system, the human friction which had been building for almost ten years, heated to homicidal proportions.

The misfit, who turned out to be a psychologist, reduced the friction by using humor and encouragement. Ultimately, it became clear that crewmembers on the first two expeditions, after ten years of close confinement, had simply killed each other, causing their spacecraft to crash.

A few weeks after I read that story my family took a two-week driving trip from Los Angeles to Seattle and back. It was a long trip for my mother, father, younger brother, and me. I loved vacations, but even an occasional Sunday drive back from a friend's house often ended with my father screaming at David or me for some real or imaginary transgression. I was sure that on our journey to Seattle it wouldn't take more than a few days for our family friction to heat us to the boiling point.

But this time, as we loaded our suitcases into the trunk of our turquoise Desoto, I decided that I would be our psychologist, our clown, the "little bit of oil" to ease the friction.

Our trip was a notable success, even when, one afternoon, my father locked the Desoto, leaving his keys in the ignition. I helped him fish them out with a wire coat hanger, alternately encouraging him and trying to be funny.

In a different circumstance I've learned that when a friend is feeling sad, the best "oil" I can provide is to listen and sympathize. I don't have to solve a problem—time will do that.

With proper lubrication a car engine will last for many hours of use. With proper lubrication from humor or from just plain listening, a human relationship will run smoothly for many years.

TIP THE MESSENGER

Nobody likes the man who brings bad news.
—SOPHOCLES
Antigone

The applause of a single human being is of great consequence.
—SAMUEL JOHNSON
Boswell, *Life of Johnson*

Why do so many of us pay attention to the news? Why do we enjoy gossip or surf the Internet? Simple—to find out what's going on in the world outside of our skin.

Why are the avenues of social media so popular? On Facebook we post and comment on photos, movies, or fashions. We tweet our daily movements. We Evite to arrange a get-together.

Many of us send and receive a large number of messages every day. Heck, in writing this book I'm a messenger myself—I'm sending messages to you.

Way down deep each of us wants to survive, to thrive, and we must realize on some unconscious level that information helps us to do just that. We read about epidemics around the world and worry about catching some fatal disease. We see the stock market soar and wonder if it's too late for us to invest for a profit. We ask our kids how they're doing in school—and whether they are succeeding or failing we should encourage their honest reply. For whatever reason, each of us seeks and receives a lot of information from other people.

If you want to keep that information flowing in, you should make it a practice to Tip the Messenger.

Karyn, my office assistant, just came in to tell me that a check I had expected was not in today's mail. My first instinct is to ask her, less than pleasantly, "What do I have to do to get checks here on time!" I can go from zero to exasperation in a nanosecond. Of course, if I show my anger I will punish the messenger, and next time Karyn will think twice before giving me "bad" news. The best way for me to cut off my supply of information is to offend the messenger. The best way for me to keep those cards and letters coming is to Tip the Messenger.

"Thank you, Karyn." A "thank-you" is always safe. "Please find out where it is as soon as possible, and let me know."

"Sure thing," and she hurries off to locate that missing check.

The wife of one of my close friends used to ask him every evening to tell her what happened during his day. When she heard something she didn't like she sounded critical.

"You had lunch with WHO?"

It wasn't long before he began to censor his news flashes because he wanted to avoid her criticism. I can tell you this now because they are no longer married. When I am the messenger I prefer to be rewarded. Don't you?

When one of my children called to tell me he was in an auto accident my first reaction was, "Are you OK?" After all, shouldn't that be my most important concern? I want my children to ask for help when they're in trouble, so I praise them for telling me when they have a problem. I know a woman who always first asks her children, "What did you do to cause the problem?" They don't come to her with their problems because she criticizes them as messenger.

You can always choose how you respond. You can kill the messenger with censure, or pull out that verbal twenty-dollar bill as a reward. When you tip generously, the messenger will soon return with more messages.

PEOPLE **33** TOOL

CATCHING A FEATHER

The softest things in the world overcome
the hardest things in the world.
Non-being penetrates that in which there is no space.
Through this I know the advantage of taking no action.
—LAO-TZU
The Way of Lao-Tzu

Her drama was a drama not of heaviness but of lightness.
What fell to her lot was not the burden
but the unbearable lightness of being.
—MILAN KUNDERA
The Unbearable Lightness of Being

When we were kids, my brother and I had the mother of all pillow fights. It ended with a shriek of glee when David swatted me squarely on the top of my head. His pillow burst, liberating thousands of feathers into the air. For weeks afterward gypsy bits of white fluff roamed through our house, rising from dresser drawers, drifting out of folded clothes, and even, to my surprise, peeking out from the corner of a small red carton of cloves in the kitchen pantry.

But each time I tried to trap one of these feathers with my hand it fluffed away. At first I was amused, but soon I became frustrated. One rule I then lived by—"go for it"—simply didn't work. My pure aggressiveness was not the best option. You have to wait for the fish to bite.

Those floating puffs proved that the chase can drive away the catch. Darn! To catch a feather I had to be patient, reach out, and simply wait for it to land, or not, on my outstretched palm.

Recently my business partner, Harvey, cornered me in my office.

"Alan, I have a problem."

"What is it?"

"My son, your godson, Byron. He and I had an argument about the rules in our house, and he won't talk to me."

Byron is twenty-three years old and his father's pride and joy. As far as I knew their relationship had never been tarnished by any significant conflict. But my experience is that at about age sixteen or seventeen children need to move away from their family of origin. They leave as children, return as adults. Harvey's quarrel was about Byron and his girlfriend sleeping in Byron's bedroom overnight, with Harvey's seven-year-old stepdaughter in the house.

"Alan, I don't want to lose my son. But I won't change the rules in my own house. What can I do?"

I recalled the day many years before when my own teenage son Steve had decided to live with his mother rather than accept one of my household rules. Eventually I had apologized to Steve, not so much for the rule but for my harsh way of imposing it, and we reconciled. In my mind I saw a feather gradually floating into my hand.

"Don't chase him," I said to Harvey.

"Don't chase him?"

"Just put out your hand and wait."

"I have been waiting. For a week. And it hurts."

"Waiting can be the hardest thing in the world, especially for people like you and me who are used to going after what we want. Children have to stake out their own territory. At some point you can't help, and they won't even let you get in the way. The only thing you can do is wait."

Harvey shook his head.

"I don't like it, but you may be right." He looked sad.

For several weeks, Harvey held out his hand. He left welcoming messages on Byron's telephone answering machine. When Byron finally returned his calls, Harvey made it clear that he was available to meet. Finally, after more than a month, father and son shared dinner at a Chinese restaurant. Harvey told Byron how sad he was that Byron couldn't abide by the house rule, which Harvey would not change.

During the next few months their dialogue continued intermittently.

Last Friday, Harvey raced into my office, beaming.

"The feather has landed. Byron has taken a job in Australia for the next three months. He leaves in just a few weeks." Harvey paused for dramatic effect.

"Yes?"

"And tonight he's coming to the house for dinner, for the first time since Christmas!"

I hadn't seen Harvey grin so broadly since he had announced his engagement to Joanie several years before, but that's a feather off a different bird.

To catch a feather you have to wait. You can't speed up the natural process of floating, and the very attempt will push away the object of your desire.

You can only be available, as you might be to a newborn infant who cannot talk. You can open your heart and turn your palm upward toward the sky. You can wait and watch with yearning and generosity.

When the feather alights you can give thanks for a precious gift. If unseen forces push it from you then wish your dream well and set your sights elsewhere.

You might also realize that, from time to time, you are the feather.

THE EQUAL RELATIONSHIP

Take a perfect circle, caress it and you'll have a vicious circle.

—EUGENE IONESCO
The Bald Soprano

Oh lonesome's a bad place
To get crowded into.

—KENNETH PATCHEN
Lonesome Boy Blues

I believe that every good relationship must be perceived as approximately equal by both parties most of the time. To put it another way, you have to give as good as you get, and get as good as you give, to achieve sustained mutual satisfaction.

I say "perceived" because beauty, as well as everything else in this world, exists only in the eye or mind of the beholder. Period. I enjoy listening to the piano music of Chopin. You might prefer Lady Gaga. Or silence. That is why an outsider can never know for sure how and why a relationship works, or doesn't work. A relationship is an internal process between two people.

I say "approximately equal" because exact equality is rare and unnecessary. That is where the 80% Solution comes into play. When I rate another person as meeting 80% or more of my ideal for their role in my life (friend, barber, spouse), that is good enough and I'm not looking to improve. (In the case of a brain surgeon I would probably go for 98%, or whatever is the very best available.) My life is sunny when I'm satisfied. I do not need always to search for better. So if I feel I get out of a relationship about as much as I put in 80% of the time, I am content.

You can achieve approximate equality in a relationship either by giving more of yourself or giving less. My usual tactic, if I feel I am not getting enough, is to rework the balance by giving less. If you keep the conversation superficial I will spend less time with you. This was true with my mother when I was an adult. She refused to have a heart-to-heart talk. Ever. When I was child we had wonderful conversations for hours at a time, but when I was an adult, for some reason she withdrew. After many attempts over a number of years I simply gave up and chose to spend less time with her. I felt I was getting less from her so I gave less of myself and as a result I found myself more satisfied with what I did manage to get from her.

The Equal Relationship can be attained, and often is, but it is a balancing act and can usually be achieved only if both parties are willing to work at it.

There is one significant relationship in which my usual tactic of giving less of myself to correct a perceived imbalance was useless. More than useless, it was just plain wrong. And I persisted in using it for about thirty-five years. That is with my wife.

When I was unhappy with her, I withdrew. As a result, she hid herself from me more and more. So I withdrew further. Our relationship, like many, had gone downhill until I decided, for some reason, to try something entirely different (when your tool fails time after time, abandon Patterns Persist and try something else—anything else—maybe the opposite of what you have been doing).

Rather than giving her less I finally decided to start giving Daveen more, much more. I told her that she has been my number one priority from the day we were married, more than thirty years ago.

Then we "cleared the decks" and talked about what we wanted and what we withheld. Other than in the first four years, our marriage has never been better. It's still about equal, but at a much higher level (90% instead of 40% on the Fox Satisfaction scale). We both broke out of the cycle we had been trapped in for half of our lives. And I learned an important lesson. From the start of our relationship through today I credit Daveen with indirectly encouraging me to conceive quite a number of People Tools.

If it's really important to you to get more—give more. But you have to go first. It might be worth it. And if you are in a relationship where your partner is unable or unwilling to reciprocate, then at least you'll realize the true situation and you can choose to give less or get out.

The Equal Relationship is well worth pursuing. And maintaining.

PEOPLE **35** TOOL

HONEY FIRST

You can catch more flies with honey than with vinegar.
—AMERICAN PROVERB

Whoever you are—I have always depended on the kindness of strangers.
—TENNESSEE WILLIAMS
A Streetcar Named Desire

I'm not talking here about how you treat your sweetheart. No, I'm talking about something I learned from my father, in restaurants, many times.

When we ate out, which was not often when I was young, if there was anything Dad disliked about the food or the service, he would instantly confront the waiter.

He began by waggling his index finger, with a "come over here" motion.

"You call this food warm? Here. Feel it. It's ice cold." And my dad would grab the waiter's hand and pull his fingers into the mashed potatoes, or whatever. Dad did have a way of making his point.

"I'm sorry, sir. I'll have the chef heat it up." After wiping his hand on a napkin, the waiter would pick up my dad's plate and take it back to the kitchen. It usually was not returned for fifteen minutes, and often was too hot to touch.

And I was uncomfortable, partly because I wasn't allowed to start eating until everyone could start. Now my food was getting cold. And there was Dad, just sitting at the table, glowering at the door to the kitchen. We all had to wait.

In my twenties I finally said, "Dad, I'm uncomfortable when you attack the waiter at a restaurant. It's unpleasant, and you have always said that a meal should be pleasant. So please try asking nicely the first time. You can always go from nice to mean. You can't go from mean to nice."

I like to have as many bites at the apple as I can get. When I start with nice I have more options.

For the last many years Dad has done it my way, at least when I'm around. Occasionally I have come upon Dad yelling at some hapless service person who has performed at less than Dad's high standard. I guess that he likes to get his anger out on someone who can't fight back too well.

I read a story years ago in which a woman who was a martial arts champion entered her home to find a burglar stuffing her possessions into a sack.

Immediately, she swung into action and quickly had the man up against the wall with her fingers around his neck.

"I always start nice," she said, "because that leaves me somewhere to go."

Start nice. Saying "please" helps. Use Honey First. You'll achieve better results and you'll always leave yourself somewhere to go.

LEVERAGE

Give me where to stand, and I will move the earth.
{Said with reference to the lever.}
—Archimedes
Papers of Alexandria

A companion's words of persuasion are effective.
—Homer
The Iliad

In the real estate business we often talk about "leverage." By that we mean buying investment property with as little of a cash down payment as possible. For example, if I can buy a $1,000,000 apartment building with a down payment of only $100,000, and if the property increases in value by only 10 percent ($100,000), the profit will be 100 percent on the original $100,000 investment. Of course, leverage cuts both ways. If that apartment building decreases in value by 10 percent, the investment will be wiped out. That's what happened in the 1929 stock market crash, where a 10 percent down payment was all you needed to buy shares of stock. When stock prices tumbled by only 10 percent your investment disappeared. That is also what happened in the recent Great Recession with property values falling as much as 40 percent. In particular, the value of many single family homes fell below the amount of the loan, wiping out homeowner equity.

In my personal life I like to use what I refer to as "energy leverage"—putting in minimum effort for maximum result. My parents used to call that "lazy," but to me it just made good sense. It's a lot easier to order "take-out" for lunch instead of walking to my car, driving to a market, buying groceries, driving home, cooking, etc.

But financial leverage and energy leverage, while useful, are not exactly what I'm suggesting as a People Tool in this chapter. For our purpose here "leverage" means using whatever you now have to get whatever you want, as effectively as possible.

For example, if you go to a hardware store to buy a fan you would expect to pay the asking price. If you buy ten fans you can almost certainly negotiate a discount. If you buy a hundred fans you could negotiate a larger discount. If you want to buy a thousand fans you should deal directly with the manufacturer. When you buy in large quantities you can negotiate a discount. You have leverage. You offer something the other side wants—a big sale.

A friend of mine runs a property management company. When she buys insurance for twenty-five properties she will negotiate a much lower premium than when she buys insurance for one property. That's using what you have (a large order) to obtain what you want (a lower price).

Where can you find leverage? Everywhere. Just find as many things as possible that the person or company you are negotiating with wants. If you are negotiating with me and can't find anything that I want from you, then you are going to have a tough time convincing me to do anything for you. How do you find out what I want? There are a number of possibilities.

1. Observation (Patterns Persist). I've always been overweight, so it's a good guess that I like food.

2. Projection. I probably want exactly the same things that you want: money, love, respect, convenience, fun. It's a long list.

3. Creativity. Here you just have to figure out something I might want, and then sell me on your idea. ("Have you ever been to Bora Bora? The beaches there are fabulous.")

4. Find someone who has a lot of what you want. After you figure out what I might want, don't be afraid to use your knowledge and position. Don't give your leverage away.

Sometimes you have to read subtle signals. A few weeks ago I was on the phone with the vice president of a major company with more than five hundred stores in the United States. They had a dispute with me and claimed that they had the right to pay half rent for fifteen years. I disagreed. After a vigorous twenty-minute argument their VP said, "Well, Mr. Fox, then we are going to have to talk internally about our options."

I said, "Fine. I agree. You should consider every option. To help you I'll tell you right now what I will do. If you haven't paid this month's full rent in eight days I will file an eviction action against your company for nonpayment."

This is where the conversation should have ended. But in this case the VP kept trying to persuade me for another ten minutes.

When the conversation finally ended, I turned to my general manager and said, "We won. They kept on trying to change my mind, even after their threat, which means they will pay the rent and won't litigate."

Sure enough, the next day the VP called to tell me that they were sending a check for full payment by FedEx.

For the past month I have been negotiating the sale of a major office building at a very high price. The sale seemed in peril because I would not agree to the potential buyer's final demand. Finally, this afternoon, I told my representative to give in. But in response to his call, the buyer's representative sent an e-mail saying that tomorrow morning his attorney would have his comments on our contract. That means the other side has been paying their attorney to work on the contract. I'm guessing that they will withdraw their last demands.

When you meet me, ask me what happened with that potential sale. Now I really hope I'm right.

My sixteen-year-old daughter wants to borrow my car. Hmmmm. Do you think she'll be willing to clean up her room first?

Leverage. Find it. Use it. Work it and it will work for you.

DANGLE A CARROT

She knew how to allure by denying,
and to make the gift rich by delaying it.
—ANTHONY TROLLOPE
Phineas Finn

Shape without form, shade without color,
Paralyzed force, gesture without motion.
—THOMAS STEARNS ELIOTT
The Hollow Men

What is the use of a carrot, other than to dangle it in front of a donkey to encourage him to walk toward a tempting reward?

Of course I'm talking about a metaphorical carrot—a reward—not a real carrot. So how can you best use a symbolic carrot when you interact with other people?

Dangle a Carrot works quite well in two ways.

First, it is a reward for behavior you want to encourage. Second, Dangle a Carrot can either freeze or encourage the response of another person.

First, the actual reward. Patti, a friend of mine, has a fifteen-year-old son, Damien. Patti is always on time, but each weekday morning when she drives Damien to his school bus he is late. This is a big problem for Patti. If the bus leaves before Damien arrives she has to drive him all the way to school. Have you ever tried to motivate a habitually late teenager to be on time?

I suggested that Patti reward Damien by paying him one dollar each day he is on time. (This tool is a subpart of "Catch Them Being Good.") Patti improved on the carrot by adding the stick—each day Damien is late she penalizes him two dollars. Patti tells me that for the past two months this reward/punishment system has worked well consistently. Damien is now almost always on time, and more than a few dollars ahead.

Years ago, when one of my children was struggling in school, I began a reward system for grades: ten dollars for an "A," provided that there were no grades of "C" or less. This system worked so well that all of my (six) children piled on. This reward system has been more expensive than I thought, but it has worked not only to encourage my children to raise their grade point average, but also to establish good work habits so that a reward is no longer needed. Rewards (metaphoric carrots) work. (You do have to be careful about this, however—rewards can undermine intrinsic motivation.)

How can you use Dangle a Carrot other than as a reward? The second use of the symbolic carrot is to either delay action or to encourage immediate action.

For example, I recently hired a company to repair the outside security shutters at my home. The shutters didn't move, and were either entirely shut or entirely open. This was not helpful. The work went slowly, and on Friday of the third week the work was 95 percent complete. The owner of the company visited me in my home.

"We are 95 percent complete," he said.

"That's right," I agreed, "and as I said I will pay you in full when the work is complete."

"It's Friday, and I have to make payroll today. Pay me 95 percent, and I'll finish the work first thing next week. I can't send anyone out today."

"I will pay 100 percent of your invoice when you complete 100 percent of the work."

The owner was upset. He left my house in a huff. And guess what. Somehow he found one of his workers to come to my house and complete the job that day. I immediately paid him in full. Without Dangle a Carrot the shutters might be stuck shut yet.

Perhaps you have experienced a situation in which someone has presented a bill that reflects inflated charges you did not expect. To prevent this situation, it is always a good idea to negotiate the specific terms of the work and of the payment in advance. By establishing the specific terms up front you can usually, though not always, prevent an argument later. But sometimes a dispute will arise anyway.

In these situations I don't want to pay attorneys. I want to resolve the disagreement. To do that I need to stay in contact with the other side and be clear that I will pay immediately as soon as we agree on the amount. I ask the other person to show to me how they are entitled to payment of the full amount billed. Then I might ask for backup information. Exactly who did the work, what time did he/she start and finish each day? Why did it take so long? What is the identification number and specific cost of any part used?

When I am satisfied, I pay. Until I am satisfied I Dangle a Carrot of payment.

One advantage of using the carrot this way is that occasionally the service provider sees the light all by himself and reduces the charge. A second result is that he/she may eventually settle for a more reasonable amount.

At the right time you will find it useful to Dangle a Carrot. It's a tool which motivates people to behave in a way that is appropriate.

But remember that when someone dangles a carrot in front of you, you should recognize the situation and press for a quick resolution. You don't want to wait for long without taking action.

A HOUSE UNDIVIDED

A house divided against itself cannot stand.
—ABRAHAM LINCOLN
Speech at the Republican State Convention,
Springfield, Illinois [June 16, 1858]

If you can't stand the heat, get out of the kitchen.
—HARRY S. TRUMAN

The People Tool of A House Undivided means that the structure of your life will hang together best when you are consistent. Take a position and maintain it. This is especially true when dealing with your small friends and occasional nemeses: your children.

Years ago I was staying with my brother in his rented condo overlooking the Golden Gate Bridge. My cousin Beth stayed with us for several nights. At 8:00 p.m. the first evening she began to put her three-year-old son David to bed. I intentionally said "began."

"Go to bed, David," she said. Then, after a pause, "Okay?"

I was surprised. Here was an adult asking the permission of a three year old to put him to bed. She invited an argument, and needless to say she got one. The house was divided against itself. There was an order ("Go to bed") and a retraction ("Okay?"). I think her son finally went to bed an hour and a half later, after much yelling, several cookies, at least two trips to the bathroom, and having upset me and, I presume, every other adult in the room, including Beth.

My children know well that I value education. I have told each of them that I will pay for as much education as they want to profitably pursue.

At age seventeen my son Steven gave me ultimate bragging rights by becoming a freshman at Harvard University. Two years later he dropped out for the second time.

"To get A's I would have to work all the time, and if I don't do that I'll get C's," he said. "I'm not willing to work that hard, and I'm not willing to get C's."

I had no problem with Steven's dropping out. I have seldom been able to force myself to work hard at anything I really don't like. But I did have a problem when he called me a few months later.

"Dad, I'm thinking of living in Berkeley," he said.

"Great! I love Berkeley. I look forward to visiting you there."

"I wouldn't be going to school. Just living there."

"Great, Steven."

Then he came to the point. "Uh, Dad, would you pay for my apartment and car expenses?"

I didn't have to think about that for more than an instant.

"No."

Silence. "Why not? You paid my expenses when I was at Harvard." My kids all know how to debate. In our family it's a survival skill.

"Steven, when you were going to college, that was your job. I paid you to do your job. You quit your job, you don't get paid."

"Oh." Our conversation ended on an unsettled note.

The next day Steven called back. The debate continued.

"Dad, I figure that you were paying me $8.50 an hour to go to college. I can't earn more than $5.00 an hour at a job."

"Gee, Steven, maybe you quit a pretty good job."

Steven did move to the Bay Area and lived with his girlfriend's family for a year. He took two jobs: delivering the *Wall Street Journal* in the early morning, and working as a bus boy in a restaurant during the day (he was later promoted, as I recall, to short order cook).

After a year or so he announced that he was enrolling at the University of Washington.

"Great," I said, "but this time you have to continue each semester until you get your bachelor's degree. If you drop out again I'll love you, and I'm sure we will have a great time together, but I will never again pay for your education."

Steven agreed. Sure enough, in November of his senior year he called me. He was depressed, not enjoying his classes, and thinking of dropping out.

"No problem, Steven. But if you drop out I will never again pay for your education."

"Just checking."

The House was Undivided.

Steven stayed in school and completed his bachelor's degree in physical oceanography. Then he earned a master's degree in atmospheric physics. After that Steven entered Dartmouth Medical School and completed his MD degree. Before his final year of medical school Steven and his new wife lived in London for a year, where he earned a second master's degree—this time from the London School of Health, in tropical medicine. Now he's finishing a PhD in public policy.

Talk about paying for an education! Now Steven threatens to go to law school or, at least, cooking school. He has let me off the hook, however, and says he will pay for his own education in the future.

I believe that my consistent position about paying for Steven's education helped him to complete it. Several times over.

A House Undivided means that you are consistent. You know your needs and your limits and stick to them.

APOLOGY

Faultless to a fault.

—ROBERT BROWNING
The Ring and the Book [1868-1869], IX,
Juris Doctor Johannes-Baptista Bottinius, l. 1175

Never apologize and never explain—it's a sign of weakness.

—FRANK S. NUGENT and LAURENCE STALLINGS
She Wore a Yellow Ribbon (1949 screenplay),
spoken by John Wayne

My goodness! Here we have the poet Robert Browning suggesting that someone who needs to appear to be perfect is flawed, and the actor John Wayne telling us that we should never show weakness by giving an apology. Robert or John: who should you go with on this? Should you, like my dentist, apologize quickly and often when you hurt someone, or should you hang tough like an attorney I know and never admit the weakness of a mistake?

I use the People Tool of Apology thoughtfully, but I do not apologize under all circumstances.

First, we need to recognize that John Wayne (or his writers) may have been thinking that an apology is an admission of fault, and therefore an admission of weakness. I respectfully disagree. Each of us makes small or large mistakes every single day. I know that I do. If I forget to take my cell phone with me in the morning I have made a mistake and I am at fault, but why should I apologize? Who should I apologize to (other than those who call me unsuccessfully)? Actually, I do apologize to Daveen when she brings me the errant phone.

My point is that I do not apologize merely because I am at fault. I apologize to soothe another's ruffled feelings, sometimes even when I don't believe I'm wrong. Why not? An apology takes very little time or energy. So let's get rid of the idea that an apology equals weakness or an admission of fault. I don't think that my dentist ever intends to hurt me. I think he wants me to feel as good as possible about the painful experience of having a cavity filled.

The actor Kevin Kline in the movie *A Fish Called Wanda*, found himself required, in his own self-interest, to apologize. As much as he tried, he found it almost impossible to say the words, "I'm sorry." I found that scene very funny, but oh, so true. Words of apology tend to stick in the throat, or in the mind, or somewhere in between. Let those words out!

An easy example happened two days ago, when Daveen woke up quite sick. "I'm sorry you're not feeling well," I said in the morning darkness. She did not blame me for her temporary illness. I did not feel in any way responsible. But I did want her to feel better, so in this case my "I'm sorry" was an expression of support and not an admission of fault.

But suppose I was at fault. Suppose I had been sick first, and insisted on coughing all over the place, contaminating bedding or other surfaces. In other words, suppose Daveen, rightly or wrongly, thought that my selfishness or carelessness caused her to catch her illness from me? I would say, "I'm sorry you're sick, and I'm sorry that I wasn't more careful." The benefit of my apology is that Daveen will feel better, she will feel supported, and she will feel to some extent that she is not responsible for her own pain. What do I lose? Maybe she'll be angry with me for infecting her, whether I did or not, but I would rather she feel better from my apology than that I think of myself, probably incorrectly, as blameless.

In 1999 or so I read a book titled *Do I Have to Give Up Me to Be Loved by You*, by Jordan and Margaret Paul. The basic idea is that when an intimate partner asks you to change something ("I would like you to wash your hands before dinner") you have two choices:

1. You can have an intent to learn. ("Why is washing my hands before dinner important to you?")

2. You can have an intent to defend. ("I washed my hands before I left work.")

In my experience an intent to learn, which may end in an apology, leads to agreement and good feelings between two people. By contrast, an intent to defend almost always leaves the other person feeling shut out and angry. As a practicing pragmatist I find that there has never been a downside when I have apologized, and there has seldom been an upside when I should have but didn't.

I would be delighted if you use the People Tool of Apology to help yourself and others. If not, well, I'm sorry this isn't a tool that will work for you.

AFTER YOU, GASTON

Gratiano speaks an infinite deal of nothing,
more than any man in all Venice.
His reasons are as two grains of wheat
hid in two bushels of chaff:
you shall seek all day ere you find them,
and, when you have them,
they are not worth the search.

—SHAKESPEARE
The Merchant of Venice

Let us alone. Time driveth onward fast,
And in a little while our lips are dumb.
Let us alone. What is it that will last?
All things are taken from us, and become
Portions and parcels of the dreadful Past.

—ALFRED, LORD TENNYSON
"The Lotus-Eaters," Choric Song

Early in my business career I supervised the management of as many as eighty-four apartment buildings in the San Fernando Valley, a suburb of Los Angeles. It seemed to me that whenever I visited a building the resident manager would ask me for something. "We need to paint the doors," "The parking lot has to be resealed," "I'm going on a vacation for two weeks and need someone to fill in for me."

After a year or more of this I began to feel like a piggy bank which my resident managers wanted to raid every time they saw me. In many cases, of course, they were right. In many cases I disagreed. In some cases they were right but we just didn't have the money to spend.

How did I respond? I usually said that I would "think about it." I sometimes scribbled a note to myself as a reminder. Occasionally I followed through, but more often I didn't. This led to telephone calls repeating the request, taking a great deal of my time and theirs, not to mention causing a great deal of mutual frustration.

Finally, I found a solution to separate the wheat of need from the chaff of want.

"We need to acid wash the swimming pool," says the manager.

"Please put your request in writing and send it to me at the office," say I.

My response produced two immediate benefits. First, I didn't have to take any notes. Second, 95 percent of the time I heard nothing more. I figured that if it wasn't important enough for me to notice in the first place, and if it was not important enough for the manager to put in writing (in those days before the miracle of e-mail), then it wasn't important enough for me to spend money on.

I call this the "After you, Gaston" People Tool because it is based upon the idea that I will do something only after you do something. In other words, you have to go first.

There is a second and perhaps even more important application of After You, Gaston in everyday life.

Very often a friend will ask me for advice. If I can answer immediately, I will. But if I would need to spend an hour or two to help, I give my friend a homework assignment.

"You asked me whether or not you should buy the house you just looked at in Santa Monica. While I know a lot about real estate, I do not have any current information on that particular market. I would be happy to take a look at the house with you, but first I need from you a write up of three or four houses which you have actually seen, the price asked, and your thoughts comparing the house you prefer with those other alternatives. Also, please let me know how long each house has been on the market, and at what price the broker thinks the house you like will sell. Send me an e-mail today or tomorrow, then we can set up an appointment for both of us to inspect your new house."

Usually I receive what I ask for. In that case I can either advise my friend immediately ("The price you think will buy the house seems like a bargain—make an offer a little lower, and let me know. I can take a look once you have a deal."), ask for more information ("What are the assessed valuations for property tax purposes on all of the houses?"), or go out with my friend and take a look at the house.

The important principle here is that my friend must help me, and invest more time in his project than I do. Tom Cruise in the movie *Jerry Maguire* puts it this way: "Help me help you."

A variation on this theme took place when my son Craig was hired as a professor in the business school at Duke University.

"Dad," he said, "I got the job at Duke, so it looks like I'll be moving to Raleigh Durham. I'm going there in a few weeks, and I would really appreciate your helping me select a house."

"That's great, Craig. Let's coordinate dates. I'd love to spend a few days with you getting to know the area, and giving you my ideas about the houses you look at."

Two weeks later Craig and I spent two days with a real estate broker looking at houses. At the end of the first day Craig said, "Dad, you haven't given me your opinion about any of the houses. What do you think about that last one?"

"Craig, I think that the most important factor is that you must love the house. If you don't love it, don't even consider buying it. If I like it and you don't, you shouldn't buy it. If you love it and I don't, then you should go ahead. My opinion about the house may be helpful on practical issues ("Did you notice the hog rendering plant next door?"). And maybe I can help you on the negotiation. But you have to pick the house first. Yourself. Until then my opinion would not be helpful."

In other words, my opinion goes second, after Craig's. (Yes, he bought a very nice home, as I recall, on one acre, a ten-minute drive from his office at the University.)

A smaller, but important use of "After You, Gaston," is helping a child with spelling. I will not even try to remember all the times one of my sons or daughters would ask me, "How do you spell X?"

I would always say, "Good question. What letter do you think that word starts with?"

When we agreed on the first letter I would ask what letter might go next. I suggested that he or she sound it out.

I found this to be an excellent teaching tool. They go first, I go second.

Is there anything else you would like to know about this People Tool?

After You, Gaston.

TRICK OR TREAT

There is a smile of love,
And there is a smile of deceit,
And there is a smile of smiles
In which these two smiles meet.

—WILLIAM BLAKE
Poems from the *Pickering Manuscript*

Oh, but he was a tightfisted hand at the grindstone. Scrooge!
a squeezing, wrenching, grasping, scraping, clutching, covetous
old sinner! Hard and sharp as flint, from which no steel had ever
struck our generous fire; secret, and self-contained, and solitary
as an oyster.

—CHARLES DICKENS
A Christmas Carol

It seems that every year around Halloween I read a story in the *Los Angeles Times* about a trick or treating child who has bitten into a nasty surprise—a razor blade in an apple or LSD in a candy bar. I didn't like to believe these stories, but as a parent I became more and more cautious about what my young children collected in their bags of tasty treasure.

I hate unpleasant surprises. This is why I am particularly sensitive to hidden agendas. Whoever inserts a dangerous substance into a Halloween treat is acting out the hidden agenda of wanting to either scare or injure a child.

Almost every working day I receive a number of telephone calls from strangers. The caller usually begins with, "Hello, Mr. Fox. How are you today."

Does my anonymous caller really care about how I feel today? Of course not. He cares about selling me something. This is a (not so well) hidden agenda, and the salesperson is trying to covertly manipulate my actions.

It is important to understand the distinction between manipulation and influence. When you want me to perform a particular action, such as helping you to move into your new house, you might use any one of a number of People Tools, but if your ultimate goal is *hidden* from me you are using manipulation.

To be forthright you might say, "Alan, Pete and Alice are helping me move next Saturday, and I would really appreciate you coming by at 9:00 a.m. to help out. We should be finished by 2:00 p.m., and I'll buy the lunch." This is a direct approach, using the tools of appreciation, social influence, and reciprocation.

You might, however, omit your ultimate goal and say, "Alan, some mutual friends are getting together at my place next Saturday, and I think you would have a lot of fun if you joined us." Notice that this time something important has been left out—that you want me to help you move. Manipulation happens when an important part of your agenda is missing.

The best tool to deal with manipulation is Question Mark. Ask for more details. "Who will be there?" "How long do you expect this gathering to last?" Most important, "Is there anything specific that you expect me to bring or do?"

Be direct and use Treat. And when someone else tries to use Trick on you, back away as soon as you realize the manipulation.

Years ago I wanted to buy a VW bus. I called several dealers, and one offered me a $1,000 discount from list. I drove to the dealership and, you guessed it, "the manager wouldn't approve that big a discount." I was foolish and bought the car at a $200 discount. Next time I'll be more specific on the phone call, and walk out if I feel they are trying to Trick me.

Trick or Treat is not confined to Halloween.

BACK OFF

Have unlimited patience. Never corner an opponent, and always assist him to save face. Put yourself in his shoes—so as to see things through his eyes." —BASIL HENRY LIDDELL HART
Deterrent or Defense [1960]. Advice to Statesman

Courage is what it takes to stand up and speak; courage is also what it takes to sit down and listen. —WINSTON S. CHURCHILL

I admit that in some ways I'm quite assertive. You don't ever want to get on my "four times a day" contact list. On the other hand, there are times when I recognize that the best tool is "Back Off."

Years ago I was driving "over the hill" on Coldwater Canyon from Beverly Hills back to the San Fernando Valley where I live. About half a mile from the top of the hill my car ran out of gas. Don't ask why, because then I would have to go into driver incompetence. And I was the driver.

I had no choice and pulled over to the side of the road. This was years ago, before cell phones existed. I needed to call my wife to get either gas for the car or a ride home. But I was still near Beverly Hills, and there were no public telephones for miles. So, as much as I do not like to rely on the kindness of strangers, I walked to the nearest house and rang the doorbell.

Since I'm a man, and I imagined that at midday anyone home would probably be a woman, I decided to stand very close to the front door, but as soon as the door opened I would take two steps back. I hoped that this strategy would indicate that I wasn't a threat.

My plan worked, with a curious twist. I walked up to the front door, rang the bell, and a woman answered. I took my two steps back, then revealed my predicament and that I needed to call my wife for help. The woman asked for my wife's phone number, then shut the door in my face. She said she would make the call. Fortunately, Daveen answered and assured the woman that I was, indeed, her husband. After that the woman let me into her home. This was a victory for Back Off.

When I was single I met Judy, a very attractive woman, and asked her out on a date.

"Sorry," she said. "I go for guys who are six-foot-three, blond, with blue eyes." I was startled.

"I could do something about the blonde and blue eyes," I said, "but the six-foot-three is about seven inches out of my reach."

I always shrink when I'm rejected, but Judy had her three requirements which I didn't fit. And I wasn't even close.

Back Off. Why waste my time and hers?

While I was in law school I fought a traffic ticket I had received for speeding. After he testified I cross-examined the officer who had given me the ticket, and I was doing pretty well. In fact, I think the judge would have let me go without a fine. But I failed to Back Off, and asked a final fatal question:

"Do you think I was driving at a safe speed?"

"Oh, no," the traffic cop answered. Since California at that time had a "basic speed law" which said that you couldn't drive faster than was safe, I lost my case by asking one question too many. Back Off, Alan, Back Off.

In my marriage with Daveen I pretty well know where she has erected a few solid brick walls, those protective walls that, after years of huffing and puffing, I cannot blow down. So, even though I like to "win" every argument, when I run into one of those walls I Back Off. Why fight for another half an hour when I know all that will happen is that I will run out of breath and both of us will end up angry.

When up for their annual salary review my experienced employees will ask me if I'm in a bad mood that day. If I am, what do they do? Right you are! They Back Off. "Tomorrow or next week would be fine."

My instinct is to forge ahead. But remember—there are also times to Back Off. That's what the reverse gear on your car is for.

THE LONE STRANGER

Once the realization is accepted that even between the closest human beings infinite distances continue to exist, a wonderful living side by side can grow up, if they succeed in loving the distance between them which makes it possible for each to see the other whole against the sky. —RAINER MARIA RILKE
Letters

The day after that wedding night I found that a distance of a thousand miles, abyss and discovery and irremediable metamorphosis, separated me from the day before. —COLETTE
Noces

Seventeen years old and in love. What could be better? Twenty-one years old and married to Jo Anne, my high school sweetheart. Still in love. What could possibly be better?

Twenty-eight years old and thinking about the possibility of divorce. What changed in those seven years? Colette might call me a slow learner.

One way to think about what changed is simply to say that we grew apart. There was more distance between us. But what, exactly, does that mean?

Years ago I read an interesting book which talked about cultural differences. Apparently each culture has invisible rules about how far apart people should stand when having a conversation, and this book stated that in most Middle Eastern cultures people stand quite close when talking. They can inhale each other's breath. Americans prefer more distance. The English stand farther apart than Americans. This conjures the comical picture of an American talking to an Englishman, who consistently backs off as the American advances in order to be closer.

It's important to note here that there is no right or wrong. If both people agree, they can stand two inches apart, or two meters (for non-Americans). It makes no difference to me.

But it does make a difference to them. Let's suppose that you and I are talking and you want to stand close to me but I want some distance. So we do the dance—I back off and you advance. Which distance is going to prevail? Unless you back me into a corner from which I can't escape, the two of us will end up at the greater distance. Whoever wants the greater physical or emotional distance in a relationship will win every time. If you disagree, think about your own relationships, present and past. If you wanted greater distance did you get it? If not, did you (will you) leave?

Why is that important? Because there are many distances in a relationship. There is emotional distance, psychological distance, self-disclosure distance—the list is long. You have to realize that we seldom think about distance in the various dimensions of our relationship. For example, suppose you want to talk to me on the phone four times a day but I prefer to talk with you once. We'll probably end up talking once. You will be dissatisfied because you want more, and I may be unhappy because, while I'm getting the distance that I want, I will feel pressured by you for more. If we are unaware of our differences, or cannot ultimately reconcile our needs, we are doomed to be chronically dissatisfied with each other until and unless one of us makes a change.

This is exactly what happened in my first marriage. After seven years I wanted more disclosure, more honesty, greater mutual exploration of our emotional needs. My first wife didn't want to go there.

Her need for more distance prevailed. We've been divorced for more than forty years. If you find yourself in a relationship where there are differing needs, and what relationship does not, you must first decide if you can live with the difference. If not, and you don't want to either change yourself or do the "dance" forever, you might need to accept that it is time to move on.

It's no fun to be a Lone Stranger.

PEOPLE 44 TOOL

HAVE A NONVERSATION

He knew the precise psychological moment
when to say nothing.

—OSCAR WILDE
The Picture of Dorian Gray

Magnificently unprepared
For the long littleness of life.

—FRANCES CORNFORD
Rupert Brooke

In certain areas I am a slow learner, and arguing with my wife is one of them. After many years of a successful marriage Daveen and I had still not quite mastered the art of arguing constructively. Too often our arguments end with both of us unsatisfied. I withdraw in anger and despair and she withdraws in hurt, each of us entrenched in the same position we started with.

If you have never had this experience, either you have never lived with someone for a long period of time, or you and your partner are much better at resolving your quarrels than my wife and I have been. But as Daveen and I had the same arguments, and the same unsatisfying results, I realized we needed a better tool. Our arguments only produced more anger and withdrawal, which simply continued the problem.

As discussed in Apology, when your significant other complains to you about his or her favorite subject—you—you can have one of two responses: Intent to Learn, or Intent to Defend.

"You left your dirty underwear on the bathroom floor. Again."

Intent to Defend: "No I didn't." Or, "You left your shoes in the bedroom where I tripped over them. Again." Or, "You should have picked them up for me, like I do for you." Or, "Don't you remember? You told me to leave them on the floor of the bathroom, because I always miss the hamper." Or, "I was in a hurry." The list is limited only by your imagination, and every single entry on that defensive list will serve only to make the problem worse. (Unless, of course, there is no problem—you, or your spouse, or both of you simply like to fight. Maybe that seems natural and perfectly okay. If so, skip right now to the next chapter. I don't want to spoil the fun of your fighting, and I'm serious about that.)

Intent to Learn: "Thanks for pointing it out. I'll put my underwear in the hamper right now. Can you help me figure out a way to remember better in the future?"

But even in the best of relationships, the landscape of an argument can be difficult to navigate. For more than twenty years Daveen and I have argued about how to argue, and specifically how to use Intent to Learn effectively. Perhaps this is a small problem, but it certainly has been long lasting. And it is a problem for which I have struggled to find a useful People Tool.

When I have a complaint my impulse is to complain. What could be more obvious? And yet it has been a completely unproductive way to resolve a dispute with my wife, especially if I wanted an apology or change in her behavior. From the beginning I am destined to fail because my complaining results in Daveen becoming defensive and denying either the problem, her part in it, or both. To prepare for the inevitable conflict I start out belligerent and I end up even more belligerent. Of course, Daveen would say that I was extremely defensive myself. Maybe she is right, but I am the writer.

Recently I discovered a way to take the "D" out of Defensive.

Now, instead of no conversation, or a *Fahrenheit 451* conversation, we have a nonversation. This means that one of us tells the other his or her complaints, with no response expected or, indeed, allowed. Either I talk or Daveen talks. Only one of us has a turn today. No explanations, no answers, no promises. Just listening. I don't have to start out angry, because I know that she is not going to be defensive or tell me I'm wrong, because she isn't going to reply at all.

"Alan, I get scared when you are two hours late getting home from work. And when you came in the door you were more than two hours late."

A nonversation. I listen, and I say nothing. (No Al Gore or George H. W. Bush here, no cheating by making a face or looking at your watch. Just listen.) No explanations, no answers, no promises.

You can often get your message across more effectively in a nonversation than in a conversation. Then, just maybe, the light bulb will forget about being defensive and want to change in the future. At the very least you or your partner will feel heard, which is important in itself.

So after many years Daveen and I have finally found a constructive way to break ourselves out of the cycle of hurt, anger, and defensiveness. Using the tool of Nonversation, we can say what we need to say without falling back into the unproductive, perhaps unconscious, patterns of our past.

Enough said. I know you've been listening. But you get a turn, too. Let me know if you have a question or disagree.

PEOPLE 45 TOOL

SNIP

A time to get, and a time to lose;
a time to keep,
and a time to cast away.

—THE BIBLE
Ecclesiastes 3:6

As to the Adjective: when in doubt, strike it out.

—MARK TWAIN
Pudd'nhead Wilson

Many years ago I read a book by Harry Brown entitled *How I Found Freedom in an Unfree World*. The essence of his advice was that when a relationship is over you should let it go and provide room in your life for the next relationship that, for him, was always better.

I don't believe that the next relationship, or next anything, is always better than the last, though it certainly has that possibility. I do believe, however, that just as in a tropical rainforest (I'm traveling in Central America at the moment) unless a tall tree falls its tiny successor will never be bathed in full sunlight. In other words, you have to make room for your future.

If your life and relationships are now perfect, please turn to another chapter and come back to this one if and when you need it. If, however, you would like to create space or sunlight in your life for a new experience or person (see the 80% chapter), then consider "Snip." Cut out that which is not working for you.

In the 1970s, heyday of "encounter groups," a woman joined our ongoing group. She was forty-five years old and had held the same job for twenty-five years. She hated her job, and had for a long time. The rest of us suggested that she simply quit, but that was and is much easier said than done.

When you Snip a job or person out of your life, you are left to encounter the fearsome black hole of the unknown. Often you have to simply accept your fear of the unknown. Or you can plan. When in school you swing on the playground rings, you always have to grab the next ring before you loosen your grip on the current ring. That is where two hands are useful. The woman from the encounter group ultimately resolved her fear by looking for and finding a different and better job before she quit the one that she was so unhappy with.

In the quote at the beginning of this chapter, Twain is encouraging us to eliminate the unnecessary. As writing teachers often advise, "Kill your babies." A word, thought, paragraph, or entire chapter—each may be beautiful, but if it doesn't belong, doesn't add to the total, then Snip. This applies to real life just as it does to writing. This People Tool has been difficult for me to use in my writing, not because I love all of my babies, but because I don't like to waste anything. I have invested time and thought to write ten pages. When I throw them out I grumble that I have wasted my time. Then I remember Sunk Cost, and Snip.

Of course, the opposite is true. With Snip I hope I have created a better product so that you will not lose interest or waste your time. And though my goal is always perfection, I seldom achieve it on the first try, if ever. When I write, I want to do my best, and the 80% Solution is not good enough.

Karen, another woman in that same encounter group, on one fine day called all four of the men she was dating, and ended each relationship. Quite a day's work. The Big Snip. But she had decided that she wanted to find a more meaningful and committed relationship and by eliminating the men who did not fit the bill she certainly created a lot of space to find the one right person.

I encourage you to do the same. If it isn't working in your life (be it a relationship, a job, or an adjective), then Snip and make room for something which may work better.

PEOPLE
46
TOOL

TRUE COLORS

Appearances often are deceiving.
—AESOP
The Wolf in Sheep's Clothing

One finds many companions for food and drink, but in a serious business a man's companions are very few.
—THEOGNIS
Elegies, I. 115

Eight months ago I loaned $10,000 to—I'll call him Boris (not his actual name). Because Boris leads a tangled financial life the actual promissory note was signed by his wife Catherine (not her actual name). Boris, or Catherine, was late in paying me back. They had given me a number of supposedly valuable Chinese antiquities as security, as well as a deed of trust on real estate.

At the time of the loan I decided not to record the deed of trust because the title company said there were many previous liens and I wanted to save Boris the cost of the title policy. I also thought that the value of the Chinese bowls and jade carvings he had delivered as security were probably more than enough to pay the loan.

At this point I'm not going to comment on my own stupidity in loaning Boris and Catherine the money, because Hindsight is not a tool which I recommend. I am much more concerned with The Power of Prediction—making a good decision in the first place.

When the loan was not paid on time I did record the deed of trust. A week later Boris called. It seems that Catherine was putting a new loan on the real estate and that my deed of trust would have to be paid first. That was fine with me.

When the new loan funded I received the full amount due, plus interest. Boris promptly demanded that I return his remaining collateral—the Chinese stuff. I told Boris by phone that I would happily return his bowls and carvings to him but I would need a receipt and a release, signed by both Boris and his wife. I prepared the document and when Boris showed up I asked him to sign it. He said he would, and he faxed a copy to Catherine for her signature. I asked my assistant to follow through and let me know the instant we received Catherine's faxed signature, so that we could give Boris the property and he could be on his way

This wasn't good enough for Boris. After about five minutes he harangued me with, "I don't have time for this 'rich guy shit' you're pulling on me. I'm taking my stuff now and leaving. Catherine will sign and send you her signature when she gets around to it."

With that he grabbed the three bowls and two jade statues off my desk and began to leave.

"Wait a minute. You need to sign the receipt," I said.

He turned back, angrily signed, and stalked out. His true colors, dark and ugly, billowed through the air behind him.

In this book I've already talked about the Belt Buckle: believing actions when they conflict with words. In True Colors I am suggesting that you believe the words that predict future action.

Let me be clear. When he asked me for the loan Boris was sweet, understanding, and considerate—in a word, persuasive. It turns out that Boris is a guy who, when he wants to make a good impression, puts on sheep's clothing. He looks good in it, and he certainly fooled me.

But today he squarely punched one of my buttons. When I do someone a favor and he or she becomes belligerent I become angry.

I did Boris a big favor. He thought that with my loan he could buy into a treasure trove of antiquities that he could sell at a huge profit. He was angry because he actually had to pay me back (my deed of trust was unexpectedly recorded against his real estate) and he probably had no intention of repaying me. Or maybe he was angry because I insisted on a receipt signed by Catherine, but the last thing I needed was to give Boris the property and have Catherine later sue me, claiming that the collateral really belonged to her. From my perspective I've been a reasonable, nice guy, and have gone out of my way to help Boris out. And yet Boris reciprocates by cursing at me in my own office.

I immediately resolved to use True Colors, and never have anything more to do with him.

Of course, True Colors can also be beautiful. Years ago there were serious fires in the hills behind my home. Seeing the fires on TV, two of my friends immediately called me to offer their homes if my family had to evacuate. I still remember their kindness.

Each of us is complex. As Walt Whitman observed, "Do I contradict myself? Very well then I contradict myself, I am large, I contain multitudes." Are you capable of great sorrow? Great anger? Moving from one emotion to the other in an instant? Probably. But one test, perhaps the best test, of your true character, or mine, is found in what we do, or say, under stress. As Lucretius wrote more than two thousand years ago, "So it is more useful to watch a man in times of peril, and in adversity to discern what kind of man he is; for then at last words of truth are drawn from the depths of his heart, and the mask is torn off, reality remains" (*De Rerum Natura*, book III, line 55).

Boris revealed colors true enough to last a lifetime. I learned my lesson, and have acted accordingly. I suggest you do the same with the people in your life. The better you know them, the more true their colors become.

GREEN GRASS NOW

You don't know what you've got 'til it's gone.
—JONI MITCHELL
"The Big Yellow Taxi"

*There's no place on this earth where I'll belong when I'm gone . . .
so I guess I have to do it while I'm here.*
—PHIL OCHS
"When I'm Gone"

In 1969 I hired Jessica as a legal secretary for our two-man law firm. Jessica worked for me, on and off, until 2011, when she retired.

In the early days Jessica seemed to live by the maxim "The grass is always greener on the other side of the fence." Her husband was a soldier in the Vietnam War. "As soon as he gets back, my life will be better." Then he returned. "As soon as we have a baby, my life will be better." And she had a baby. "As soon as we move out of Los Angeles, my life will be better." And they moved. "As soon as I come back to Los Angeles, my life . . . "

Yes, the grass can always seem greener in another field. Perhaps we yearn for more and different. Perhaps we just refuse to be satisfied with the here and now—which, of course, is all we really have.

After I bought my first house I examined the classified ads to see if I had really bought the right house at the right price. Unfortunately, most of the homes advertised in the newspaper seemed to be better homes at a cheaper price. I finally did learn the "code." "Room for a pool" meant "You might be able to put in a narrow lap pool if you use the entire back yard." "Estate-size lot" meant the same as "Junior Suite" at a hotel. Neither is the real thing. "Needs some TLC" meant that the place was a wreck.

So is the grass in the next field really greener than the grass, and weeds, in your own backyard? Does a friend's spouse seem more desirable than your own? Does the other lane on the freeway always seem to move faster than the lane you are in? Was everyone else in high school more popular than you?

To quote Shakespeare, "There is nothing good or bad but thinking makes it so." Write that one down. I live by it.

Jessica was going to be happy when her husband returned from Vietnam. Not exactly. Then she was going to be happy when she had a baby. Not exactly. Then she was going to be happy when they moved to Charleston. Not exactly.

I've talked to Jessica many times since she retired, and I am happy to report that she now seems thrilled to live in the "now." She sleeps as late as she likes, visits her grandchildren often, and works part-time when she wants to. Jessica finally appreciates the green grass in her own field.

Back in the 1970s I participated in many encounter groups, popular in Southern California at the time, in which we would encounter each other's angels and demons, mostly demons. Many of these groups were supportive and constructive. Some were attacking and destructive. I experienced both.

One exercise still sticks with me.

I was asked to write down the most important person or thing in my life. I did. Then I wrote down the second most important person or thing. Then the third, until I had a list of the ten most important people, things, or activities, in my life.

Next I was asked to imagine the tenth item disappearing. That was sad, but not devastating.

Then, the ninth. The eighth. I experienced the fantasy of losing each of the top ten anchors of my life.

By the time I imagined #1 vanishing, I cried. I was too emotional to even feel embarrassed at the tears flowing down both of my cheeks. The entire group became a circle of tears. Each of us lived in a separate but connected world of grief for about five minutes.

Then the leader asked us to imagine #10 coming back into our lives. Then #9.

By the time I reclaimed #1, whatever it was, I felt euphoric.

This was one of the most interesting half-hour journeys of my life: from OK, to devastated, to euphoria. What changed?

Almost nothing. No one had died. Nothing had actually been taken away. No person, activity, or thing had actually come into my life or left me. What changed?

Everything changed. My outlook. My appreciation for the beautiful grass I walked on every day.

And I realized that all I treasure—my wife, children, friends, home, writing—will vanish one day, if only when I die. And then, like Phil Ochs, I will not be able to appreciate . . . anything.

The grass right now is green. Really. Studies show that a year later those who win the lottery are no more happy than before they won. Nothing changed permanently. Other studies show that a year after a person is permanently disabled he or she is almost as happy as before the injury. Those suddenly disabled learn to live with their new situation, and don't fall to pieces. I used to worry about whether my life would be worth living if I lost my sight. That was an open question in my mind when I was in my twenties. Today I would persevere.

Might your grass be greener in the future? Perhaps. But if you really think about it, take a measured look. You should find that your grass is pretty green today.

Green Grass Now.

PEOPLE
48
TOOL

FALL BACKWARDS INTO
THE HANDS OF FATE

*Take me up into your mind once or twice before I die (you know
why: just because the eyes of you and me will be full of dirt some
day). Quickly take me up into the bright child of your mind.*

—e. e. cummings
The Enormous Room

*He either fears his fate too much,
Or his deserts are small,
That puts it not unto the touch
To win or lose it all.*

—JAMES GRAHAM, MARQUIS OF MONTROSE
"My Dear and Only Love"

One of the exercises which was popular in encounter group days,
and which I performed myself only once, was to fall back into the
arms of other members of the group. The exercise was billed as a
matter of trust. Now I believe these are called "trust falls."

Let me be clear. I believed that the members of the group who
stood in back of me sincerely wanted to catch me. I did not question
their desire to break my fall before I broke my head on the floor. I
only slightly questioned why this particular group encouraged me to
go first. The part of it that concerned me was their ability. There I
was, a full 220 pounds, falling backwards into the arms of six or seven

men and women who, as far as I knew, might be weaklings. They might accidentally drop me. None of them looked like a bodybuilder or fireman.

I fell backwards anyway. Isn't peer pressure grand?

Did they catch me? Yes. It was a little sloppy but, as my wife often says, a good airplane landing is one you can walk away from.

Would I do it again? Yes, but only with trained and strong catchers.

OK. So what is my point? Here I am, encouraging you to fall backwards into the arms of fate and I admit that I'm more than a little scared to fall backwards into the arms of friends.

But maybe falling backward doesn't scare you. That is my point. You can choose the part of your fate which doesn't scare you, or scares you least, or when your goal is so important your fear doesn't matter. (How about jumping from a cliff to save your life, as in *Butch Cassidy and the Sundance Kid?*)

I can easily write down a list, starting with those areas in which I have no fear, and going all the way down to those areas in which my fear paralyzes me. And guess what? At the top of the list—no fear—would also be my greatest successes. Money has never scared me, and that is an area in which I shine. And what would be at the bottom of my list? Activities I have never tried (sky diving, for example) or places I have never been (war zones).

Let's test that theory.

I say flat out that, for whatever reason, I'm not afraid of money and never have been. I'm not saying that I don't think about it a great deal, or that I don't have concern. I certainly plan and budget frequently. I am saying that once I have assured myself as much as possible with planning and research that the potential result will be favorable, then the always possible failure doesn't scare me.

As noted in a previous chapter, my former law partner and I, at my urging, used to buy rental houses and apartment buildings, then sell them to clients. I often found myself agreeing to make a down payment of $2,000 or $5,000 in thirty or sixty days, having no specific source. I didn't know where the money was going to come from. I was falling backward into the arms of fate, but financial fate always caught me and I never lost a single purchase because I couldn't raise the cash.

Please note that I do not recommend jumping out of an airplane without a parachute. From time to time even fearless mountain climbers perish. I would not do a "trust fall" if no one was standing behind to catch me.

After about two years of buying real estate, my partner Jim succumbed to his fear. He could not get comfortable falling backward into the arms of the money fate. Jim left our law partnership, and I went into the real estate business with Harvey who, like me, didn't exhibit any fear around money. Harvey and I formed a real estate company on March 1, 1968, and we are partners and share offices to this day. Need I say that our net worth is a lot more than it was when we started?

I'm not big on making actual lists, but if you think about where you thrive in life, my guess is that you will find in yourself very little fear. So use this tool to help you discover those areas in your life where you have the least fear. And then Fall Backward into the Hands of Fate, prudently, wherever you wish.

PEOPLE TOOL 49

IF YOU WANT TO KEEP A SECRET, DON'T TELL ANYONE—ESPECIALLY YOUR PERSONAL TRAINER

Three may keep a secret, if two of them are dead.
—BENJAMIN FRANKLIN
Poor Richard's Almanack

It's not me who can't keep a secret.
It's the people I tell that can't.
—ABRAHAM LINCOLN

I was sitting on the floor of my living room, stretching my body by touching my toes under the watchful eye of Lonnie, my personal trainer. My wife Daveen came in with my cell phone.

"For you," she said.

I took the phone, but as I was talking I heard Lonnie say to Daveen, "I hear you're going to Telluride."

Now what's so bad about that? Simple information. "I hear you're going to Telluride."

The problem is that I had planned a trip next Wednesday to Telluride as a SURPRISE twenty-fifth wedding anniversary gift for Daveen, and I had gone to considerable effort to keep our destination secret.

I only made one mistake. Last week I told Lonnie. I also told him it was a secret. He remembered the first part of the information, but not the second.

I fell back on the floor, and shouted some expletive to Lonnie. Daveen says she hasn't had such a good laugh in a long time.

This tool is a simple one. If You Want to Keep a Secret, Don't Tell Anyone—Especially Your Personal Trainer. Maybe your hairdresser is okay.

CLIMB A MOUNTAIN

It is not the mountain we conquer, but ourselves.
—EDMUND HILLARY

Keep close to Nature's heart ... and break clear away, once in a while, and climb a mountain or spend a week in the woods. Wash your spirit clean."
—JOHN MUIR

When I was in my early thirties I went backpacking for the first and, as best as I can remember, the last time. My friend John talked me into it.

John loved the outdoors. I loved to look at the outdoors from the shelter of the indoors. John liked to walk. I liked to sit. John thought the best meal was heated over a campfire. I thought the best meal was heated by a chef in a fine restaurant. I don't know how John talked me into a three day hike into the high Sierras, but he did.

I remember our first day out. I huffed and puffed as we ascended a trail which was child's play to John, but difficult for me. We criss-crossed a stream several times—John held my hand over the slippery parts so I wouldn't fall in.

Our first evening we camped by a lovely mountain lake, John caught several fish for dinner, and I cooked them over our small butane stove. Yes, John carried the stove and other heavy stuff in his backpack. I carried my sleeping bag, clothing, and a part of our food

173

ration. At night, my head cradled by pine needles, I looked up into a starry, starry night, shivered in my sleeping bag, and woke up often, gasping for breath, because I wasn't used to sleeping at an altitude of nine thousand feet.

The next morning at breakfast John pointed to a nearby mountain peak.

"Let's climb up there today," he said.

I looked up. Was the man crazy? That was a mountain peak. A real mountain peak. It wasn't something people climbed. It was something people drove to, parked their car, and, from the lookout, admired the view.

"John, I'd be happy to stay here today while you climb the mountain," I said. "Uh, do you think you can be back by sundown?"

He laughed.

"Alan, it's not more than a two or three hour hike."

"To the top?"

"Yes, to the top. And we can slide down, so that won't take more than an hour. We can be back in time for lunch."

Obviously, John didn't understand that a mountain was not something to be climbed, and certainly not in two or three hours. But once again, he was persuasive, and promised me that he would be happy to climb at my pace, rest as often as I needed to, and turn back at any point if I didn't want to go on. I trusted John a lot (and I still do).

We walked up the switchbacks slowly, first to our right, then to our left, resting at the end of every other one. I was sure that we would never make it to the top, but it was a beautiful day and John didn't seem to mind resting for fifteen minutes after walking for ten.

Suddenly, to my surprise and delight, we were at the top. There was nothing higher to perspire to.

"We're at the top," I announced.

John just looked at me as if I was some sort of peculiar mountain squirrel.

"I mean, we actually made it. And it only took two and a half hours."

John smiled. I don't think he had broken a sweat.

We explored that mountain top for more than an hour. Each vista was better than the last. Then, indeed, we slid down the mountainside on loose rocks, back to our campsite in time for lunch.

I've climbed more than a few mountains since, both literally and figuratively. But that was the first time I actually tried something at which I was pretty sure I would fail.

I accomplished something I had thought impossible for me. I also learned that I could complete a task I feared, with the help of a good friend.

Once in a while, do something you are not accustomed to, or something you fear. Be sure to get all the help you need. Climb a Mountain.

HOLD ME

This is my simple religion. There is no need for temples; no need for complicated philosophy. Our own brain, our own heart is our temple; the philosophy is kindness.

—DALAI LAMA

"That best portion of a good man's life,
His little, nameless unremembered, acts
Of kindness and of love."

—WILLIAM WORDSWORTH
"Lines Composed a Few Miles Above Tintern Abbey"

I live in a house at the end of a cul-de-sac. Years ago I was driving home from work in the late afternoon when I saw a two-year-old child sitting on the curb, crying. I am not drawn to young children, but I am drawn to help those in need. I stopped and approached the toddler.

From what I could understand, his name was Bobby and he lived in a house at the end of my street. Someone had dropped him off, but not at his front door, and certainly not in the care of an adult. I took Bobby home with me and offered him a glass of milk and a cookie. In twenty or thirty minutes the police were able to contact one of his parents.

If you told me that you had this experience I would question either your memory or your credibility. Yet this happened. To me. And to this day I do not understand how anyone old enough to drive a car could ever leave such a young child alone on the side of a road.

Of course we take care of our children. But it is equally important for any society or community that we also take care of each other. And when we take care of each other, the gift is magnified when care is delivered with kindness. That is why Hippocrates wrote that some patients get well only through the goodness of their physicians.

We need each other. Suppose I arrive at my office tomorrow morning and my dedicated staff of thirty-five has disappeared. I would have a serious problem.

We thrive in our lives in large part because we are able to rely on each other. This is true even when we don't personally know the people on whom our well-being depends.

I don't know where the electricity for the city of Los Angeles comes from, but if it stopped right now I wouldn't have much luck recharging either my laptop computer or my cell phone. Or in filling my car with fuel. Gas pumps rely on electricity, and we all rely on many nameless people to provide virtually everything. Who runs the water system? The sewer system? How does food travel from field to supermarket shelves? How are traffic signals maintained?

But of equal or greater importance than being able to depend on each other for our livelihoods and physical well-being is the need we all have to be connected emotionally, especially though kindness.

This is what gives us joy.

After I had separated from my first wife I gave a presentation one evening to a group of prospective new clients. Three or four members of the audience approached me afterward to ask a few questions about real estate investments and express interest. I was elated, until I began the long drive back to my sparse apartment. Who could I share this good news with tonight? Chilly sheets?

It is our sustained connection with each other that gives our lives meaning.

Let's each use the People Tool of Hold Me, both literally and figuratively, to enhance every life on the planet. Be kind. It works, perhaps better than any of us can ever know.

PEOPLE 52 TOOL

A MILLION MILES AWAY:
FOCUS ON THE PROCESS
AND LET GO OF
THE OUTCOME

Attachment is the great fabricator of illusions;
reality can be attained only by someone who is detached.

—SIMONE WEIL
Gravity and Grace

What one knows, in youth, is of little moment;
they know enough who know how to learn.

—HENRY BROOKS ADAMS
The Education of Henry Adams

From a million miles away I cannot see myself. I am small to the vanishing point. Up close I blot out the sun and the stars.

When I was a young attorney, all too often I received bad news in the mail. A letter from the Internal Revenue Service, a complaint from a client, the notice of a loss in court—any one of these would instantly ruin my day.

As time passed I realized that while unpleasant news might destroy a single day, three days later the same news simply blended into the background of my life, losing all of its initial influence over my mood.

After a number of years I established a firm rule for myself to let distasteful news simmer in the stewpot of my psyche for two or three days until it was a part of the whole, but not my whole life itself.

Ultimately I refined this rule, and taught myself to be attached not to outcome, but to process. I do the best I can, and trust that whatever happens will be for the best. I think of this as taking a longer perspective than I used to.

A few weeks ago I wanted to buy a limited edition car. I learned that there was more than a year-long wait for delivery, but that one buyer had died and his car was immediately available. I contacted the dealer, signed a contract, and was promised that the car would be mine as soon as my deposit was received. Later the same day I was told that there was another, slightly higher offer for the same car, and that the first wire deposit to be received would win. I immediately instructed my bank to wire funds early the next morning. At 6:00 a.m. the next day I telephoned my banker, and urged him to send the wire at once.

Later that morning the car dealer told me that the other deposit had been received twenty minutes before mine, and that I could not buy their car. This didn't stop me for a moment. I began to look for another similar car, and discovered one that would better meet my needs. And it is a color I like better. Now, if the first dealer calls to tell me that their other sale has fallen through, I wouldn't be interested.

John, the friend with whom I climbed a mountain, once told me that he had worried about many things in his life, most of which had never happened.

While it is difficult to not treat everything in my life as up close and personal, I realize that from the perspective of time very little is truly important in and of itself. I do what I can. The result is the result.

I cannot see myself from a million miles away. I am small to the vanishing point. I think I'm better off that way.

Buddhists call this letting go of attachment. I think of this tool as the ability to be A Million Miles Away: Focus on the Process and Let Go of the Outcome.

PEOPLE 53 TOOL

UNEVEN STEPS

Look to the essence of a thing, whether it be a point of doctrine, of practice, or of interpretation.

—MARCUS AURELIUS ANTONINUS
Meditations

I went to the woods because I wished to live deliberately . . . and see if I could . . . learn what it had to teach, and not, when I came to die, discover that I had not lived.

—HENRY DAVID THOREAU
Walden

Daveen and I had set aside the final day of our vacation in Jerusalem for last-minute shopping, but before we left our hotel the telephone rang. It was Adam, a biblical scholar and our tour guide. For two weeks he had shepherded us through the ancient monuments and unfamiliar philosophies of a timeless land.

"You must explore today the historic excavations south of the Old City," he insisted. We agreed to meet him at the Western Wall in late afternoon, not knowing exactly why.

I was born in Los Angeles in 1940. To me any building older than I am is an historical monument, but in the Holy Land the concept of "old" takes on an entirely new meaning. Here nothing was "old" unless it had existed for at least twenty centuries. During our travels in Israel we had stood at the mouth of a verdant valley. Adam claimed it was the exact spot where David slew Goliath. We climbed to the top of the partially excavated walls of Jericho, a site that humans have inhabited continuously for ten thousand years. We viewed the Dead Sea from the high and ancient fortress of Masada.

It turned out that Adam's reason for drawing us back to the Old City of Jerusalem at the twilight of our stay was not archaeological. After squinting up at great stone walls and peering down into the depths of vertical shafts which I thought of as earthen time tunnels we found ourselves standing at the base of the southern steps to the Second Temple, which was demolished almost two thousand years ago.

"Notice something unusual about these steps?" Adam asked. During our days together he had frequently challenged us with a question like this. Coincidentally, the night before I had read about these very steps in our guidebook.

"Uneven," I said.

"That's right! Why is that? Were the people who built the Second Temple just careless? Did they use a bad contractor? Have the steps become uneven over the passage of time? Ground settled? Earthquakes?" Adam loved to share his personal distillation of ancient wisdom.

"So that we would think," I said. Adam had quoted the Old Testament throughout our travels. His opinions usually differed from those in our modern guidebooks, but this time he agreed.

"Yes. Most steps are even. You wouldn't want to trip on the stairs while carrying a morning cup of coffee up to your bedroom. And you don't want to have to pay attention to each individual step every time you enter a building. But those who built the Second Temple wanted each person who came here to slow down, to think before he acted, and to delve into the essence of his life and what he could learn here."

Essence. Was that the reason Daveen and I had flown from Los Angeles to Jerusalem, survived on airline and hotel food for almost two weeks, and abandoned our final shopping spree? Was the ultimate reason of our journey simply to stand on these uneven steps— to slow down and pay attention? Was the heart of my life simply to be mindful?

As Adam, Daveen, and I huddled together on those venerable stairs, brushed by the clamor of distant traffic, caressed by the silence of eternal dusk, I knew that life, at its core, is simple. At the center of the most elaborate puzzles in life there sits a truest truth, the essence of the matter. I recalled a meditation class in which I had spent twenty minutes eating a single raisin.

Later, in gathering darkness, we three descended the two-thousand-year-old steps of the Second Temple, paying attention to each stride as the ancient builders had intended. With each step I felt, perhaps like Thoreau, that in these few moments I had truly lived.

Pay attention to all of life's Uneven Steps.

THE ROAD

*The prologues are over. It is a question, now,
of final belief. So, say that final belief
must be in a fiction. It is time to choose.*

—WALLACE STEVENS
"Asides on the Oboe"

*I shall be telling this with a sigh
Somewhere age and ages hence:
Two roads diverged in a wood, and I—
I took the one less traveled by,
And that has made all the difference.*

—ROBERT FROST
"The Road Not Taken,"
Mountain Interval

It is almost time for us to say good-bye. There is one remaining thought that troubles me. It has troubled me since the beginning. It is a question you may have asked yourself.

"How shall I choose which tool to use in a given situation?"

I could clothe my answer in many words, but I prefer the simple tool of Honesty.

My answer is, I don't know. Experiment.

Does this leave you back where you started? Not at all.

I hope that this book has expanded your vision, that you will see doors where your sight has been blocked by walls, and that you will know the comfort of partitions where before you have been nakedly exposed in open space.

In short, I hope that this book has awakened your mind and heart to alternatives. It is a beginning, not an ending.

What have I learned in writing this book?

1. Writing a book is a lot of work and is rewarding but not always fun.

2. People Tools pervade my life more than I had thought.

3. Human possibilities are virtually limitless.

4. The opposite can be more effective than the customary.

5. I don't know all the answers. I don't even know some of the most important questions.

Three hermits lived together in a cave. One day a palomino horse ran by.

Two years later the first hermit said, "Sure was a pretty white horse."

Three years after that the second hermit said, "Twasn't white. 'Twas golden."

Five years passed before the third hermit announced, "If you two are going to talk so much, I'm leaving."

THOUGH ISOLATION MAY BE AN INSEPARABLE PART of the human condition, I invite you to share your People Tools experiences. Talk to your friends. Let me know what tools work best for you. What helpful People Tools have you discovered for yourself?

Let us keep in touch, and share the road we travel by. When we experience joy in our lives, what else do we really need?

ABOUT THE AUTHOR

© Gregg Segal Photography

Alan C. Fox has enjoyed a number of lifetimes during the past seventy-three years. He has university degrees in accounting, law, education, and professional writing. He has been employed as a tax supervisor for a national CPA firm, established his own law firm, and founded a commercial real estate company in 1968 that now owns and manages more than seventy major income-producing properties in eleven states.

Alan is the founder, editor, and publisher of *Rattle*, one of the most respected literary magazines in the United States. He is also a practicing pragmatist. He sits on the board of directors of several non-profit foundations. *People Tools* is the distillation of seventy-three years of his experience in accounting, law, real estate, poetry, three marriages, and raising six children, two step-children, and one foster child. *People Tools* is Alan's way of giving to you the benefit of his thought, experience, successes, and mistakes.

We are each human, with all that label implies. *People Tools* will help you make the best of a life, which is, alternately and simultaneously, both ridiculous and sublime.

You can visit Alan's blog at Peopletoolsbook.com, or contact Alan directly at alan@peopletoolsbook.com.

You can also:
Like Alan on Facebook: www.facebook.com/PeopleToolsBook
Follow Alan on Twitter: @AlanCFox